HAIR COLOUR IN THE HORSE

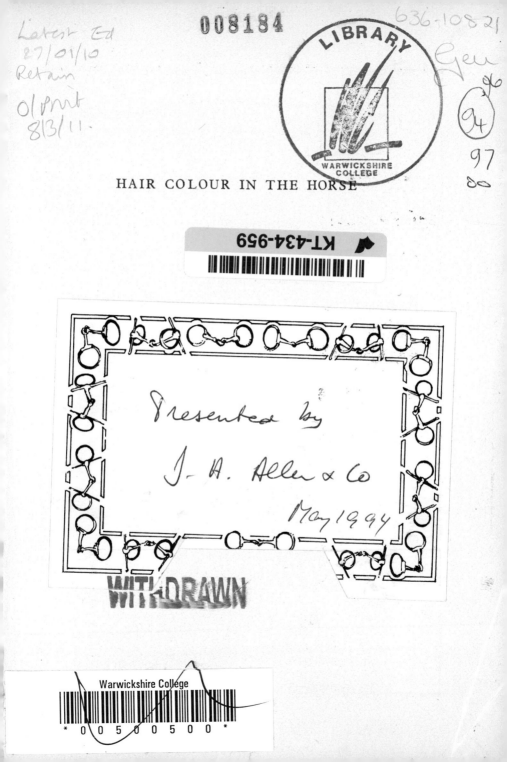

Presented by

J. A. Allen & Co

May 1994

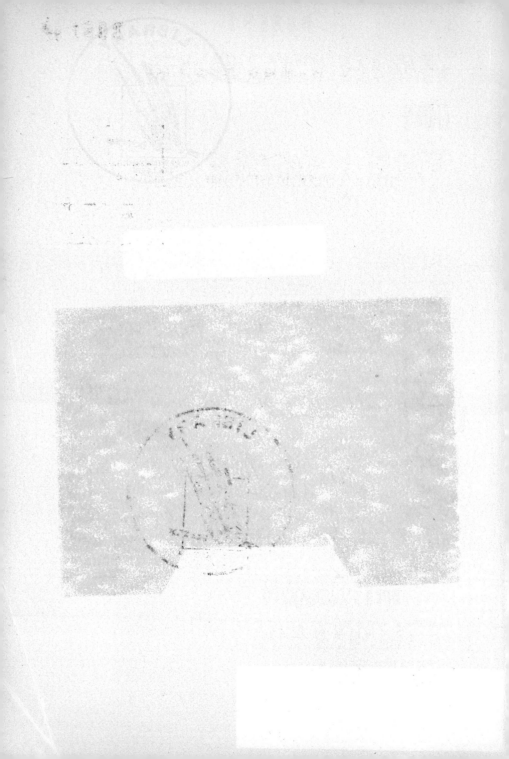

HAIR COLOUR
IN
THE HORSE

R. GEURTS

TRANSLATED BY ANTHONY DENT

J. A. ALLEN
LONDON

Geurts, Reiner
Hair colour in the horse.
1. Colour of horses   2. Horses – Genetics
I. Title   II. Dent, Anthony
636.1'08'21   SF291   77-30127

ISBN 0-85131-290-X

First published in Holland. This first English translation published
1977, by J. A. Allen & Company Limited, 1 Lower Grosvenor Place,
Buckingham Palace Road, London, SW1W 0EL

and at
Sporting Book Center, Inc., Canaan, N.Y. 12029, United States of
America.

Printed in Great Britain.

CONTENTS

5

LIST OF ILLUSTRATIONS

PLATES

7

FIGURES

TABLES

INTRODUCTION AND DEFINITION
OF TERMS

FOR A long time there has been an overall conception of the heritability of coat colour, or the basic colours, in horses. But now that breeders have come in contact (principally in the context of the Welsh pony) with a greater range of colours than the traditional bay, black and chestnut, it is desirable to look more closely at the ideas and hypotheses concerning their occurrence. These are derived from the study of the genetic background. In this book we shall follow principally the views of W. Castle, one of the authorities in this field.

This has led us to divide the work in chapters, not according to colours, but according to the genetic factors which are regarded as determining the coat colour in horses. At present not much is known about this, so that for an answer to many questions one is dependent on information derived from comparative genetics and the study of coat colour in other species. Add to that, that research on horses costs a great deal of time and money due to the long interval between generations and the small number of progeny, in comparison, for instance, with rodents. A population study on the basis of stud book data can be of some help, but only to a limited extent since the data are so often incomplete and not reliable.

We shall not go into the simple Mendelian theory of splitting and regrouping, which is valid for most colour genes, and whereby the outcome of a mating, for instance bay × black, can be forecast. Knowledge of this is deliberately assumed, but it seems useful to give a résumé of the most important principles of genetics insofar as they come into play in the inheritance of coat colour.

In the matter of usage about genetic symbols, there is unfortunately no uniformity. The most convenient way seems to be to take the school of Castle as the point of departure. Neither can we dispense with a description of the more important coat colours under the names now current. The vocabulary now in use for this purpose has been greatly simplified in comparison with that formerly used, which was more fanciful, and there has thus been a considerable gain in clarity.

TECHNICAL TERMS USED IN
THE SCIENCE OF GENETICS

chromosomes

genes

loci

allele
mutation

genotype

phenotype

gametes

homozygote

Visible, at a certain stage in embryonic cell division, as rod-shaped sections, built up of coloured layers which are regarded as bearers of hereditary factors, or genes (unit factors). Chromosomes also contain less distinctly coloured (heterochromatic) parts, which some consider to be reservoirs of inactive genes. Loci are the places, or positions, inside each chromosome occupied by individual genes. In this locus, a gene may be interchangeable with another form of gene, or allele, functionally different from it. Mutation is the name given to the sudden changing of genes. In the cells of the body chromosomes, and hence loci, are always present in pairs. Genotype is the totality of genes present in a body, the genetic composition of the individual. Phenotype is the outward and visible form (conformation, colour, etc.) of the individual, which is the product of the effect of the genes plus the effect of the external environment (feed, climate, etc.). Gametes are sex cells. By the union of two of them which have the same allele (A or a) at a certain locus, an individual is conceived, in which the allele is doubly present (AA or aa). The individual is then said to be homozygote for that allele. It can only form A-gametes or a-gametes, and is said

	to be pure for that allele. Heterozygote is when
heterozygote	the two gametes have different alleles (A and a)
	at the same locus. A heterozygote individual is
	mixed for genetic purposes. It will produce, in
	forming sex cells, half A-gametes and half a-
reduction	gametes. Reduction in this technical sense is

heterozygote

reduction

dominant

recessive

dominant

intermediate

interaction
epistasis

hypostatis

to be pure for that allele. Heterozygote is when the two gametes have different alleles (A and a) at the same locus. A heterozygote individual is mixed for genetic purposes. It will produce, in forming sex cells, half A-gametes and half a-gametes. Reduction in this technical sense is the halving of the total number of chromosomes which result from this during meiosis. In general, we refer to a mutant allele by the symbol for dominant (a capital letter, for example, A-) whenever it differs from the original gene in any respect in heterozygote form. But in particular a factor is dominant when it is completely expressed in heterozygote form, so that individuals which are heterozygote and homozygote cannot be externally distinguished from each other. The symbol for recessive is the use of a small letter (for example, a). Recessive alleles have no effect in the single form, but only come into play in homozygote form. A gene is incompletely, or partly, dominant when, for example, the appropriate characteristic for gene A is less strongly developed in the heterozygote Aa than in the homozygote AA: or when it is externally expressed in a phenotype that is intermediate, standing half-way between the external appearance of the genotypes AA and aa. Alleles of one pair, can influence each other in their effect, but so can alleles of different pairs of genes. This is called interaction. One of the forms of non-allelic interaction is epistasis. An epistatic (covering) gene masks the phenotypic effect of another gene. The latter is then called hypostatic (covered). The epistatic gene can be dominant. So that a G-grey horse that has turned white may not show what colour it was originally. But an epistatic gene can also be recessive: albinos, which are homozygous for the recessive c-allele can be invisible (cryptic) carriers of all colour factors. We see another form of interaction in piebald genes. Here, different genes which each cause a minor degree of piebaldness can so strongly influence each other that a completely white phenotype is produced. Factors which need each other and thus can only act in combination to give rise to a certain characteristic, are called complementary. The effect of a gene which influences more than one characteristic is called pleiotropic. Often a characteristic that shows quantitative variability is determined by the working together of several pairs of genes (polygenes) which each separately have a small effect. Within each pair of genes the effect can be intermediate or dominant. When these genes reinforce each other (work additively), we speak of cumulative polygeny or homomery. Cumulatively collaborating genes, however, often have effects of very variable strength, so that besides a principal gene, which prominently determines the development of a characteristic, one can distinguish modifying genes which occur as subsidiary genes, or modifying genes. Most frequently these stand together, as the undivided residuary genotype, in opposition to a pair of principal genes. Penetration of a gene means the frequency of occurrence of the characteristics belonging to it, or the percentage of cases in which the characteristics of a given genotype become apparent in the phenotype. The strength, or degree, of development of such characteristics is known as expressivity. Genes

cryptic

complementary

pleiotropic

polygenes

additively

modifying

penetration

expressivity

13

which are found in the same chromosome and are, thus, inherited together are known as coupled. Besides gene mutations, changes can also occur in large structures. Through rupture of the chromosome, symmetrical parts can be exchanged between chromosomes of one pair. Such exchanges are called "crossing over", and can lead to the partition of coupled genes. In translocation, part of a chromosome tears loose and attaches itself to another chromosome. Translocation between a chromosome of one pair leads to doubling of chromosome parts, and thus to duplication of genes. Consequent on a double rupture in a chromosome there can occur inversion (turning round) of a part of the chromosome whereby a modification takes place in the normal arrangement of gene locations. When this change is conspicuous in the phenotype we speak of a positional effect. The establishment of several mutant alleles of the same single gene, which thus by definition all belong to a given locus, and are mutually interchangeable at this locus (following Mendelian law) has led to the concept of the multiple allele or allelomorph series. Within such a series there is usually a gradual ratio of dominance, as regards the effect of the alelles. Meanwhile it has been possible to deduce from this phenomenon of crossing over, that in different series the alleles are pseudo-alleles as they can be found in the same locus simultaneously, and such loci must be regarded as complex loci. Chromosomes of one pair are called homologous. We also speak of homology between genes when they deploy the same effect in different species of animals. This homology is an important concept in comparative genetics. The proof of

coupled

"crossing over"

translocation

inversion

positional effect

multiple allele
allelemorph series

pseudo-allele

complex-locus
homology

14

homologous genes depends *inter alia* on comparison of coupled genes, on the occurrence of like allelomorph series, on the identification of an uniform effect of certain recessive factors in crossing of nearly related animal species, and on the identification of an uniform pleiotropic effect of these genes; in regard to coat colour on the comparison of the influence which genes have, for example, in transplantation experiments with foetal skin graft within and without the species.

A gene cannot always be recognized as dominant, or recessive, by the canons of classical genetics. These are very strictly defined and always have relevance to the phenotype. In the case of piebald factor series it will be apparent that alleles sometimes are not wholly recessive but neither are they (strongly) dominant, and they show only slight expression in the heterozygote. These alleles may be conceived of as conditionally dominant, because their expression depends on the totality of the modifiers present, and, above all, on other effects, among them selection. By further selection and progressive effect of modifiers, in the sense of diminished expression, they may ultimately pass into completely recessive alleles.

In the formula of the genotype, the complete dominance of an allele should always be indicated with only one capital letter, for example A-, meaning that it makes no difference to the phenotype in question whether one has to deal with the case of AA or of Aa. Partial dominance is indicated by two letters, for example Dd: the heterozygote condition, and DD: the homozygote condition; since the phenotypes are always different. In the case of a phenotype produced by the effect of a recessive allele, naturally, a double small (miniscule) letter (for example, aa) is always used in the genetic formula. Whenever two genotypes carry different alleles of one of the factors present, without its being apparent in the phenotype, only one formula is used for such genotypes. In it, the relevant alleles are written together divided by a diagonal stroke, (E/ee).

CHAPTER 1

THE ORIGIN OF HAIR COLOUR

THE COLOUR of a horse's coat and skin, is almost wholly determined by the presence, or absence, of the pigment melanin. This pigment occurs in two chemically different forms: eumelanin (black or brown) and pheomelanin (yellow or red). Both are to be regarded as grains in the bark and marrow of the hair – to use convenient terms in describing its composition – in the outer skin or epidermis, the quick or dermis or corium, the iris and other parts of the eye.

The grains are formed in the melanocyte or pigment cell, out of proteins. Their structure is regular, forming a skeleton to which the pigment itself adheres. Melanin is formed from a number of by-products, by means of enzymes arising from the element tyrosine ($C_2H_{11}NO_3$). We shall not here enter further into the nature of the chemical processes involved; and moreover, unlike eumelanin, pheomelanin is a substance about whose chemical nature very little is known as yet. We only know that the difference between the two kinds of substance is genetically determined.

In the early stages of embryonic development, the nervous system begins to be deposited by the formation of a groove in the middle of the upperside of the still more or less flat surfaced embryo. This groove quickly deepens, its side walls rise up towards each other and unite, whereby the so called neural tube is isolated from the upper surface. In the tissue dividing the side walls of the neural tube, the so called neural crest, or ganglionar framework, the primary melanoblasts (the matrix cells of pigment) develop. These move into the skin and adjacent tissues, finally ripening into melanocytes. These are cells in a condition to make granules of pigment and to expel them. (*Figure 1*).

Although the pigment in epidermis and corium, is not without im-

16

portance, the colour of the coat depends directly on the presence, or absence, of pigment grains in the hairs themselves. It is, therefore, worthwhile to enter here into the formation of hairs.

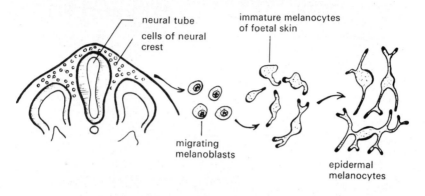

Figure 1. Development of melanocytes from cells of the neural crest.

At that stage of foetal life, when the skin already consists of three layers, of which the most important is the layer of germ cells between epidermis and corium, the formation of hairs begins everywhere by thickening and growing towards this layer. (*Figure 2* [a]). This in origination gets deeper and slowly widens out to a club-shaped outer end. As a reaction to this ingrowth, in the thickened outer end, cells from the corium begin to proliferate, which begin to lay the foundation of the hair papilla (*Figure 2b*). The involute mass of cells in the germ layer grows as one unit in depth, but is confined by the hair papilla which is forming, so that the bottom of the expanded outer end is dented inwards, like the bottom of a bottle, while the edges grow further above the hair papilla. (*Figure 2* [c]). The cells on the inner side towards the papilla form the bulb, or root, of the hair. By division and growth longways of these cells the cone of the hair, which towards its tip becomes horny and turns into true hair, consists finally of a central mass of cells, constituting marrow and covering flattened cells, the bark.

The melanocytes responsible for the pigmentation of the hair and which were already present between the cell layers of the epidermis

17

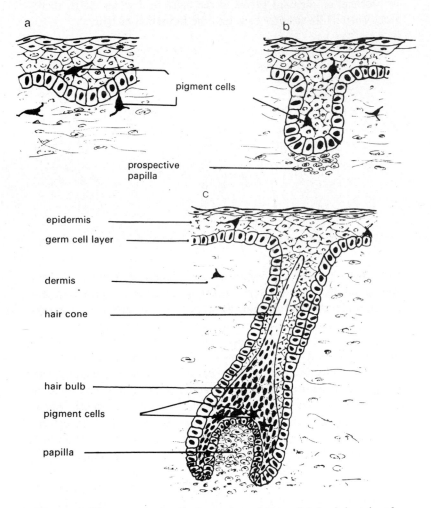

Figure 2. Three stages in the formation of hairs. (a) Incipient involution of the germ cell layer. (b) Progressive growth in depth and deposit of the hair papilla. (c) The root of the hair completely deposited and the formation of the hair-stem from bulb cells. The pigment cells have reached their final position.

18

go along with the germ cells while the hair is being formed and come exactly into the bulb in a zone just above the papilla. Here they transmit granules of pigment to the cells that will form the stem of the hair.

Somewhere in the rather complicated process that begins with the formation of the melanoblast, and ends with the production of pigment granules, the genes begin their work of influencing colour differences. This can happen through direct influence on the formation of melanin. Thus, it seems that no melanin is secreted in the granule when the production of the enzyme tyrosinase is blocked (for instance by the albino gene). Other genes limit the quantity of this enzyme. Further, genes can exert their influence on the pigment granules so that changes occur in the form, composition and number of granules, or a substitution takes place of one kind of pigment by another. To this pattern belong genes which control the changeover from the production of eumelanin to that of pheomelanin, for example. At the same time, it seems that the cellular environment, the tissue round about the hair papilla, has an important influence on the kind of pigment that the melanocyte makes. Changes of form in the melanocyte can mean that pigment granules are being formed in an abnormal way, for instance in the form of lumps, as under the influence of what is called the dilution gene in the mouse. This gives rise to a lighter colour, although there is little change in the total number of granules.

Going further back, the presence of melanocyte would appear to depend on a successful migration and a normal development of the melanoblast in the neural crest. Genes which exert their influence on the material of the cells in the neural crest, be it by inhibiting the latter in its development, or be it by hindering the proliferation and consequent migration of the melanoblasts, can cause certain forms of spotting (white patches) to occur. These markings seem mostly to be distributed quite arbitrarily about the coat. Another form of spotting can occur when the melanoblasts cannot proliferate locally, so that the pigmentation of hide and hair is confined to islands (coloured patches).

In the case of white markings in other places such as *signalements* (white socks, marks on the face, etc.), one may readily imagine that the swarming out of the melanoblasts from certain centres is disturbed, so that some parts of the skin are not reached, or are reached too late. It has been found that in mice there are eight bilateral and symmetric regions, more or less centrally placed from which the melanoblasts spread out. In this connection it is to be observed that white marks at the extremities and on the belly occur in just those parts of the body furthest removed from these pigmentation centres and from the neural crest. An effect on the melanoblast itself by attacks on the process of maturation into a melanocyte can lead to a completely white exterior or to a roan (when all cells have not been affected).

The study of inherited coat colour is concerned with all these processes; but its centre of gravity lies in enquiry into the working of genes. In the light of results obtained from rodents, among other subjects, it would appear that investigation of coat colour in the horse is still at the beginning stage. The treatment of coat colour must thus rely above all on comparative method. It is clear that this opens up a number of questions to which no answer can as yet be given, but this is inevitable.

CHAPTER 2

NOMENCLATURE OF COAT
COLOUR

THE PRINCIPLE governing the nomenclature of coat colour is that
it should reflect the impression made on the eye by the coat. This
is obviously a carry over from the past. Only fifty years ago, in the
Dutch language alone, there were some twenty terms in use to
describe various shades of bay and brown, and about thirty for
chestnut. At the present time simplification has taken place, but
the customary terms are not always in agreement with the genetic
background. Perhaps it would be as well to retain the traditional
expressions to describe shades of a colour so long as so little is
known about them. However, a certain sobriety in this matter is in
order, and terms which have no longer any practical significance
tend to fade out.

Nomenclature in English speaking countries is exclusively des-
criptive and refers to the colour of the coat at the moment when
an official description (for stud books, etc.) is noted down. As this
often happens shortly after the birth of the foal, it often gives rise
to untranslateable terms that do not correspond to the colour that
will appear after the first change of coat. This is pre-eminently the
case in the breeding of Welsh ponies, which is also intensively
carried on in the Netherlands. In cases where an exact description
of the foal's colour is difficult, it would be desirable to make a rule
that a provisional colour should be named, which can be amended
later, on final entry in the stud book. Official nomenclature in
Germany is greatly simplified (Meyer, 1949), although in a more
recent work (Isenbart, 1969) many very old fashioned terms are still
used, which are confusing and bear no relation to inherited colour.

For a better grasp of the following paragraphs, it has seemed desirable to describe the basic colours in all their shades in terms current hitherto and to define them as well as possible. At the same time we shall mention the traditional names which are likely to be met in the literature of different countries.

[The English term will be followed by the German, French, Spanish, Portuguese (if appropriate) and Dutch, in that order. But it should be borne in mind that words used to describe colours reflect a differing view of the external world from speakers of one language to those of another, even among contemporaries, and much more so historically. Thus, the Latin adjective *purpureus* does not mean the colour indicated by the modern English purple. The Old Norse language did not describe coal as black, but as blue [Kolblà]. And semantically in modern Russian, light- and dark-blue are regarded as totally different colours, not different shades of the same. *Tr.*]

Our terms will always refer to the ordinary outer hairs of the coat and the longer hairs of main, tail and fetlock.

2.1 BAY AND BROWN

The shades run from a light yellow-brown, through red-brown to a very dark-brown, or black brown. Mane and tail hairs and the lower part of the legs are black. So long as this designation (brown, or its equivalent in many European languages) refers to the colour of the mane, etc., and to colour variations of the coat consistent with it, it is not possible (except in the case of black-brown), fully to distinguish between, the bay group and the brown pattern group. It would seem desirable to do this, given the possible genetic variations between the two groups (*see Chapter 4:3*). It is possible within the English language area, where bay is not thought of as the same colour as brown. The difference is less clearly marked in French usage, according to the *Lexique International 1972*, "bai" is often used for both colours.

[I do not find this so in practice during the last three years, when I was in France: both official documents, and horsemen in ordinary conversation, speak of "bai" and "brun" in the same sense and on the same occasions as in English. *Tr.*]

The colour pattern is the best criterion to differentiate by, with the appearance of lighter shades in the coat on belly, nose and flanks: but even this is not absolute: we shall go into this in more detail later.

The following shades are still recognized in Holland, and some other countries:

Light-brown (or light bay, hellbraun, bai clair, castaño claro, lichtbruin). The coat is of a yellow-brown tint. Occasionally brown hairs are found in the roots of the tail, called in Dutch "a bloom on the tail", and more than one colour in the mane, etc. The coat is sometimes dappled and the belly notably paler in colour, as in the roe-deer and the Exmoor pony. The phrase golden-bay implies a metallic glint.

Bay or brown (rechtbraun, bai, castaño, bruin). The most frequently occuring shade of this colour.

Dark-brown (brown or dark-bay, dunkelbraun, bai foncé, castaño oscuro, donkerbruin). The darker shades, which, if a little deeper, merge into black-brown. In languages other than English, such expressions as "Kastanienbraun" are used to describe a gleam in coats of this shade: it means literally "chestnut", but has nothing to do with the English coat colour, chestnut. This effect is called mahogany in English.

Black-brown (seal-brown, schwarzbraun, bai brun/charbonné, bocifuego, zwartbruin). This is a coat so dark in colour, that it is only to be distinguished from black by the presence of lighter hairs on the flanks and a russet colour about the nostrils ("coppernose"). Here, and also in the case of bay and brown, this russet, or tan, colour can be much lighter, dun coloured, forming what is known as "mealy nose". Documents marked in English, "black *or* brown" prove that it is sometimes difficult to tell brown from black. This frequently gives rise to errors. Dark-brown horses with a noticeably lighter shade on the flanks are called seal-brown in America; in general the darker shades are all called brown.

Red-bay (rotbraun, bai cerise, castaño encendido, roodbruin).
The visual impression is unmistakeably rufous. There is little point
in distinguishing between a light and a dark (mahogany) red-bay.
The expression, "blood-bay" sometimes heard in English, refers
to this red element. Bay has always been the predominant colour of
the Thoroughbred and is the only colour of the Cleveland Bay.
Dark-bay and black-brown are popular with breeders of the Swiss
Jura, the Norwegian Gudbrandsdal, the French Comtois Draught,
and the North Dutch Warmblood (Groningen horse).

2:2 BLACK (rappe, noir, preto, negro, zwart)

Little variation is possible with this colour. The common black
that fades a little in summer, giving a drab effect, and is known in
English as rusty-black, is known in Dutch and German by names
that mean, not very logically, "summer-black". In winter the coat
is totally black, without much sheen.

Jet-black (glanzrappe, noir de jais, gitzwart). It is a permanent
deep-black coat with a metallic sheen, slightly dappled. Breeds
which are without exception black, include the West Friesian and
the Ariègois (cheval de Merens). A very high proportion of Fell
ponies are of this colour.

2:3 CHESTNUT

Chestnut is in general characterised by a varying number of more
or less red hairs and comprises a gamut of tints more extensive than
that of bay or brown. They range from a light-brown-yellow via
reddish shades to an almost black colour with a russet gleam. The
long hairs can be of the same colour, or a contrasting one, but they
are hardly ever black. At present there is a tendency to keep nomenclature simple, and we shall deal with only three variations.

Light-chestnut (sorrel, hellfuchs, alézan clair, alazão claro, alazán
claro, lichte vos). Yellowish-brown to yellowish-red, the mane etc.,
generally lighter in colour, and lighter areas under the belly and at
the extremities. The very light (washy) more yellow-brown chestnuts with an almost cream-coloured belly, known as roebuck belly

24

or pangaré, and a flaxen mane, are common among Haflingers. A rich, clear, shiny coat more like golden-dun is called, golden-chestnut or alézan doré.

Chestnut (rechtfuchs, alézan, vos). The middle tint, which occurs most frequently. The mane is of the same colour. The special terms for a richer red are, red-chestnut, sorrel, rechtfuchs, alézan cuivré, roodvos. The term, obsolete in Britain since the 18th-century, "sorrel", means in America both this colour and light-chestnut. But a chestnut even in its lightest shades is still darker than the darkest sorrel. The official *Arabian Horse Registry of America, 1970,* does not use the word sorrel, or the word brown either.

Dark-chestnut (dunkelfuchs, alézan foncé, alazão oscuro, alazán tostado). The coat is a dark-brown colour, sometimes with a grey tinge and a dingy brown/grey to very dark red-brown mane, etc., (liver-chestnut, leberfuchs). Of the innumerable shades of dark-chestnut one still meets such descriptions as clay-chestnut, meaning a dull grey/yellow red coat and mane: alézan brulé, schweissfuchs, zweetvos, meaning a grey/brown coat, slightly dappled, shiny and always with a lighter mane; grey or whitish grey: café-au-lait, coffee coloured, mulberry, kohlfuchs, alézan charbonné, alazão figado, koolvos, with a very dark blackish coat with a red glint. The mane is of the same colour.

In connection with chestnut, it is worth while to mention the occurrence of a noticeably lighter (cream coloured, flaxen or white) mane and tail, which incidentally can occur with all coat colours (*see Chapter 5:2*). Exclusively chestnut breeds, besides the Haflinger, are the Suffolk horse and the Jutland and Schleswig Draught breeds. A light-chestnut is commonest amongst American-Belgian Draught horses, and was also formerly very popular among the Dutch Draught breed.

2:4 GREY AND ROAN
Both these expressions imply the presence of unpigmented (hence white) hairs among those normally coloured. A distinction has

always been made between variable- and invariable-grey. This is not always patent from the name given, as, in some languages, the vocabulary does not suffice to distinguish them. A description "grey", *tout simple*, is not enough. It is correct to describe a chestnut horse which will turn grey as "grey, born chestnut".

Variable-grey (gris blanchâtre, tordillo, tordo, veranderlijk schimmel). The grey's coat, including the head, legs, mane, etc., is sprinkled with white hairs and eventually turns all white. Mostly the mane retains coloured hairs longer than the coat. This is also the case with the legs, especially around the knees and hocks. It is not recommended to distinguish between successive stages of the greying process in such terms as, blue-roan, iron-grey, grey-roan or dapple-grey, spiegelschimmel, gris pommelé, tordillo rodado. The same applies to the still current expression, nutmeg-grey, when the coat comprises brown, red, or yellow hairs, and flea-bitten-grey, meaning an almost-white coat with darker spots in it. Grey of this sort is very widespread among Welsh ponies and Arab horses. In France, the Percheron and Boulonnais are grey when not black.

[Probably not true of the Percheron as bred in England, hence most English people think of the Percheron as a grey horse. But from personal observation, in France for example among the stallions at the Haras National de Pompadour, the proportion of black Percherons is much higher than the "outsider" would expect. *Tr.*]

Invariable-grey, or roan (rouan, rubican, rosillo). In contrast to the preceding cases, the foal is born more or less grey, though this may only be obvious after the first change of coat. These never turn white, however, and the basic colour is always apparent. At most, the colour will bleach out a little, with advancing age. The head and lower legs, mane, tail, etc., are hardly affected at all, or only slightly. Designation is by the colour of hairs other than white, and the following are customarily recognized:

Red- or bay-roan (braunschimmel, rouan, rosillo castaño, ruão, bruinschimmel). Very frequent among Dutch and Belgian Draught horses, and the Ardennais, Trait du Nord and Auxois Draught breeds in France.

Blue-, or black-roan (rappschimmel, mohrenschimmel, noir rubican with such additions as Mohrenkopf or cabeza de moro, where the colour is more pronounced about the head).

Strawberry-, chestnut-roan (fuchsschimmel, rotschimmel, aubère, rosillo alazão, vosschimmel), is very frequent in the Breton Draught breed. Confusion is caused in Germanic languages by the use of "rotschimmel" to describe both this and red-roan. In Germany, horses which are born white are also called "schimmel", specifically "atlas-schimmel".

The presence of white hairs in small numbers, without giving an outright roan impression, is known as "ticked with white hairs", stichelhaarig, stekelharig, and is characteristic of many breeds formerly of the Dutch Draught, and even now of the Dutch Warmblood and the Noriker of the sub-Alpine region.

2:5 PARTI COLOURED HORSES (pied, pinto [American also paint], schecke, pie, malhado, pampo, pio, conjugado, bont)
[Different language groups have seen the difference between parti coloured horses in different ways. Thus, in English the chief distinction between what were originally called "bald" (in Anglo-Saxon "fag") is between piebald and skewbald as defined below, while in other languages the emphasis has been on the extent and distribution of the white areas. *Tr.*]

Piebald, or black-and-white (skewbald, or white-and-bay, brown or chestnut or even dun, pie, pie-brun, tobiano, pampo alto, pio alto). All have large and/or small white areas on any part of the body, but mainly large ones. In Dutch, this pattern is called "platenbont" or "koebont" (as in the Friesian cow). Odd coloured in English means a horse not exactly definable as piebald or skewbald, often with three colours.

27

Splashed-white (overo, pampo baixo, pio bajo). White areas of varying extent, starting on the belly, but always taking in the head, hence in Dutch "witkopbont".

(*Leopard*) *Spotted* (appaloosa, tigré, tigerschecke, tigrado, chubari, panterbont). Can occur in many patterns. The classic form consists of dark spots on a white, or grey, coat. Or even white spots on a dark coat. If these occur predominantly on the hindquarters the horse is known as blanket-spotted. It occurs in many breeds, so that the neologism Appaloosa is inappropriate as it really applies to the horse originally bred by the Nez-Percé Indians in America, who specialised in this "fancy" colour. European expressions incorporating the word "tiger" are equally infelicitous.

2:6 DILUTED COLOURS

The "pale horse" of tradition has a coat whose colour strikes the eye as washy, or diluted, by reason of pigmentary changes in the hair. Shades can most conveniently be defined by the basic colour, as:

Dun (isabel au crins noirs, louvet, falb, baio, bayo, isabelo, gateado, valk).
[Note: the Iberian terms, baio, bayo, do NOT mean bay. *Tr.*]
A dilute bay colour in various shades of grey/brown/yellow. Mane, tail and legs are black. Often there is a spinal list and sometimes zebra stripes on the legs. The coat, called in America buckskin, is a yellow-dun, and that called claybank is a reddish-dun. But there is no point in distinguishing amongst this group. Homozygosis of the dilution gene causes stronger dilution of the coat colour to a cream, or grubby, white tint. The mane, etc., are somewhat darker than the coat and of indeterminate light-drab brown or grey. This is called silver-dun or perlino.

Mouse-dun (slate-dun, blue-dun, crane, mausfalb, wolfgrau, noir mal teint, pelo de rato, grullo, lobero, muisvaal). By dilution of black, the coat in most shades acquires a grizzled-blue tinge, but often also a grey/brown gleam, quite different from the common rusty-black. Crane, in America, and grullo in Latin America, refer to a very light-grey coat, with darker mane. Mouse-dun is not always readily definable. It is possible that among horses with a grullo coat there are individuals which are really pale-dun, which is homozygote for the dilution gene.

Isabella or palomino (isabellenfalb, isabel aux crins blancs). When chestnut is diluted the coat is pale-yellow to yellowish-bay. The mane is always light-cream to white. The dilution gene in homozygote condition makes the coat cream, or off-white, called cremello, blue-eyed cream, blassisabel (formerly milchschimmel). Foals of this colour, like dun foals, are born very pale in colour. The word isabella is falling rather into disuse due to the international popularity of the palomino spreading outwards from America, where the expression implies, ideally, a coat like a new minted gold coin with white mane and tail.

Both in duns and palominos, the colour varies sharply with the seasons. Dappling often occurs in the darker palominos. Horses which are homozygote for this colour dilution gene always have blue eyes due to reduction of the pigment granules in the iris, and some British breed societies (for example, the English Connemara Pony Society) will not register foals with blue eyes and cream coats.

2 : 7 WHITE (albino, weiss, blanc, branco, blanco, wit)
Both coat and mane are white, the eyes dark or blue. True albinism does not occur in the horse, so the expression albino should be avoided. White, or nearly white, horses fall into three groups: white born greys (atlasschimmel, kakerlake) in which a partially unpigmented skin and light coloured eyes can occur; grey horses which have turned white, whose skin always remains black; and light cream coloured horses (cremellos) in which colour has been strongly diluted, eyes are blue and skin is much lighter than normal.

2:8 MARKINGS (marques, signalements, Abzeichen, sinais)
Dark marks, such as an eel stripe, or stripes on the legs, or any

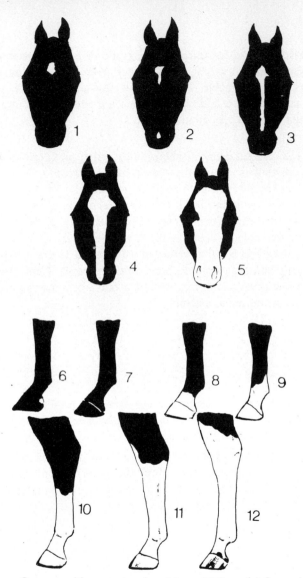

Figure 3. Some markings on head and legs. (1) Star. (2) Star with drip and snip. (3) Race, splash on lower lip. (4) Blaze right down. (5) Broad blaze, wholly white nose. (6) White heel. (7) White coronet. (8) Sock. (9) White foot running up behind. (10) Stocking. (11) White leg, running up in front. (12) White leg, over hock/knee, ermine mark.

dark mark anywhere on the coat deserve special mention. It is further customary on registration to give an exact description of any white marks. It is important that the terminology should be uniform, and simple to use. As for marks on the face (*see Figure 3*) four or five variations are recognized, not counting the faintest possible marking, which is written "some white hairs", or abbreviated "swh". These variations are:

Floret – is when the white hairs are arranged in a circle.
Star   – white spot on the forehead above the line between the eyes, which may, or may not, "drip" below this level.
Snip   – A mark in the region of nostrils and upper lip.
Blaze – This begins in the frontal region, running down the ridge of the nose, sometimes to the edge of the upper lip. If narrow, it is called a race. The horses described as "bald" in early volumes of the *General Stud Book,* had broad blazes if not wholly white faces, and this use is retained dialectically in England. According to Dreux, 1966, a blaze right down can be the result of a star and a snip growing together.

Markings are sometimes noted on the underlip, and running below the jaw. The following marks are recognized on the legs:

White heel
White coronet
Sock   – White pasterns to the lower edge of the fetlock joint. In some languages, a diminutive is used if it only comes halfway up the pastern.
White foot   – Reaching above the fetlock.
Stocking   – White halfway up the cannon bone.
White leg   – White up to knee or hock.
"Booted"   – Or the equivalent in some languages, means that the white comes above the knee or hock.

The last three markings often entail the white running up before, behind or on one side of the limiting joint, this being specifically mentioned, as also with small dark (ermine) marks in the white area, usually about the coronet.

CHAPTER 3

THE E-GENE

A FACTOR governing the distribution of eumelanin, was discovered in rabbits by R. Punnett during 1930. The cause lies in what Punnett termed the E(xtension)-gene, of which five alleles have later been discovered, while examples of this gene have been found in other species. Because they will be repeatedly mentioned later, the E-series of multiple alleles is discussed at this point, preceding the treatment of colour factors themselves.

In this series, successive dominance causes expansion and intensification of eumelanin at the expense of pheomelanin. This means that the yellow band in the normal wild (agouti) pattern of hair becomes smaller, or disappears altogether. The original gene E^+ takes care of a normal distribution of eumelanin and pheomelanin so that the agouti-pattern is fully expressed. The place next above it in the series is occupied by the allele E^s ("steel") which merely gives a partly agouti-pattern effect, manifesting itself in a steel-grey colour known as agouti-black. The most potent allele in the series, E^d (dominant) in its homozygote form makes the coat black all over. In heterozygote genotypes $E^d E$ and $E^d e$, some wild colour hairs do appear in the coat, thus proving that the E^d allele is not totally dominant.

Conversely, the recessive alleles of the series confine the formation of eumelanin and so produce an expansion of pheomelanin, more strongly as the recessivity increases. The last allele in the series, the totally recessive e-allele, causes maximum expansion of the pheomelanin so that a yellow rabbit with a white belly occurs, eumelanin being present only in the eyes.

The most important allele is E^d. This gives a phenotype that differs in no way from the black exterior produced by recessivity for

32

the wild colour factor (*see Chapter 4*). The E^d allele also occurs in rats, mink and possibly also, in sheep and cattle.

Castle (1951) supposes alleles of the E-series in the horse, and so does Odriozola (1951). But, in contrast to Odriozola who uses the E symbol for the black colour, Castle thinks the E factor can only work in combination with alleles from the A and B series. He postulates three alleles:

E^d which is epistatic when homozygous (E^dE^d) in regard to alleles of the A series, and thus totally masks the expression of the presence, if any, of these alleles; this is the cause of dominant black.

E which by a full production of eumelanin gives the coat a rich deep tint. It is thought not to mask the effect of alleles. It makes a bay horse darker bay and an ordinary chestnut, liver-chestnut.

-e which is recessive, and by the increase of pheomelanin generally produces a light coat colour. Its effect is not yet fully clarified. Other researchers, as we shall see below, give a quite different interpretation.

CHAPTER 4

THE A-GENE

THE A-GENE, which is the wild colour factor or pigment distributing factor, is so called after the agouti, a South American rodent whose fur is taken by zoologists as a typical example of the coat shades of wild mammals.

This gene in the first place limits zonal distribution of eumelanin and pheomelanin in the individual hair. The hairs in the agouti's coat have a black tip (eumelanin) and a yellow band (pheomelanin) right underneath it, while the rest of the hair is mostly grey. The transition from one kind of pigment to the other is rather abrupt and requires only three or four layers of cells in the marrow of the hair. It is apparent from skin grafts that all melanocytes from different types of agouti, dependent on the cellular environment, can produce eumelanin as well as pheomelanin. Besides this, the A-gene limits the regional distribution of pigment, that is the relative quantity of each kind of pigment in the hairs in different parts of the body, whereby those in the ventral portion of the coat are exclusively or predominantly coloured with pheomelanin pigment. Mutant alleles on the A-locus determine the width of the yellow band, which can be totally absent, as in animals other than the agouti, or can extend all over the body. In rodents in general those alleles which cause expansion of the yellow band are dominant over those which cause diminution of pheomelanin.

Undoubtedly the agouti-locus is very widespread among mammalian species, whether it be that homologous alleles, possibly under the influence of modifying genes or by interaction with other colour factors, often cause substantial phenotypic differences. In mice the A-series comprises some thirteen alleles, giving coat variations between yellow and black. The first allele, A^y (for yellow) which gives an uniform yellow coat, has probably no exact counterpart among other species. Most yellow coats are caused by recessive alleles of the E locus. The allele A^+ gives the normal wild colour, agouti with grey belly. A coat with a very light or white belly is caused by the A^w (for white) allele which occurs also in the rat and the rabbit, and possibly in the wolf, is the allele for wild colour. Another well known allele is a^t (for black-and-tan), which is also found in the rabbit, giving a coat with black dorsal and yellow ventral aspects. The a allele, last in the series, is recessive and gives a uniform black (non-agouti) coat. In mice there are indications that the A-locus may really be complex and that there are special genes which influence the distribution of light ventral, or dark dorsal, parts of the coat: in the dog there are four alleles and in the cat at least two in the A-series, or so we assume. In the dog there is a very complicated relationship between alleles of the A and E series. According to Lauvergne (1966) there are four alleles in cattle, but with a different order of dominance.

TABLE I

Conspectus of alleles in the A-series

Colour	Castle	Odriozola	Berge
Wild	A^+	A^L	A^+
Blakk	—	—	A^D
Brown	a^t	a^t	A^t
Bay	A	A^+	A
Black	a	a	a

The supposed presence in the horse of alleles of the A-gene, which here too is responsible for a given colour pattern, is a very recent hypothesis worked out in detail by Castle (1940–60) and Odriozola (1951). The ideas of these researchers differ somewhat both concerning the number of alleles and their operation, and their order of dominance, as we shall see below. Furthermore, Berge (1961) adds another allele to the series (*see Table I*).

There is no unanimity concerning the symbol for the wild colour coat, that is, what sort of coat colour the primeval wild horse had. Castle holds that this was bay, and that the "wild colour" of, for example, Przevalsky's Horse, is caused by the operation of several, possibly coupled, genes.

Here we shall proceed on the assumption that the coat of the still extant Przevalsky's Horse is the authentic wild colour, in our treatment of the different A-alleles.

4:I THE WILD COLOUR

Colour and pattern in the primeval wild horse were caused by distribution of pigment in individual hairs. The upper part of the coat was dark, the flanks lighter in colour, so was the belly and the inner sides of the legs. At the extremities (tips of the ears, lower part of the legs, and the outer ends of the long hairs in mane and tail) the concentration of pigment was higher, as in a dorsal stripe down the back, the list or eel stripe, and in the stripes which occasionally occurred on the legs and shoulders. Examples of this pattern are found in Przevalsky's Horse and in other wild living equidae in closely related varieties. It was probably also visible in the mouse-dun coat of the extinct tarpan.

Today, Przevalsky's Horse varies in colour from a light-bay to a yellow-bay with lighter patches round the mouth and nose (while the lips are bordered by a darker edge) on the underside of the belly, on the flanks and the inner sides of the legs above the knee/hock. The neck and shoulders are darker. There are often zebra stripes on the legs. The dark bay (sometimes reddish) eel stripe runs back to halfway down the tail and is continued forward in the darker mane, which is bordered on its outside by a narrow seam of lighter hairs. This last feature is not exactly obvious at all times, and is best seen in the winter coat. According to Mohr (1971) there were formerly Przevalsky horses of a darker- and redder-bay. The mutual relationship between the darker and the lighter, more yellow, coats is so far incompletely investigated. At birth, the foal is mostly very light, between orange colour and cream. Judging of the coat colour is very difficult, as colour changes not only with age, but by the season: mostly the shade gets paler with advancing age. The pale, washy, or dilute colour is said to arise from typical zone formation in the individual hairs, that is, a light part, ruddy- to yellow-white or light-grey, and a dark, black, or bay; according to Gremmel (1939) also from such a distribution of pigment granules that the inside of the hair (that nearest the skin, or ental) has fewer granules than the outer, or ectal, side. This leads to a different measure of light absorption (horse hairs are markedly oval in section). (*See Figure 4[a]*).

Coats with characteristic wild colour pattern (or any way differing from ordinary bay) whether in colour or in components such as lists or zebra stripes, are encountered among many "primitive" pony races, such as the Polish Konik, or the Carpathian Hucul, the Portuguese Sorraia or Garrano, the Skogsruss of the Isle of Gotland, Iceland and Highland ponies, the Exmoor, and many Asiatic breeds and strains in China, Mongolia and the Himalayas. The coat of the Exmoor pony is dark-bay, or brown, with a lighter belly and typical mealy nose and light patches round the eyes. The pattern

Plate 1. Przevalsky's Horse. The stripes on the foreleg are just visible. The seam of light hairs along the dark mane is not so pronounced as in the Fjord horse. (*Photo:* Wiersma).

is clearest when the winter coat is new.

This pattern is found in other equidae, e.g. in the donkey (*Equus asinus*) and the various sub-species of onager (Krumbiegel, 1958) or *Equus hemionus*. In those Asiatic races of wild ass which are still extant (khur, kulan and kiang) the ground colour is a sandy-yellow-dun to sandy-bay, while mane, tail and eel stripe are dark-brown. Nose and legs appear light-cream to off-white, likewise the belly, but with a varying degree of upward expansion along the side. This expansion is greatest in the onager, and includes even the under side of the neck and part of the thighs, while the head is almost entirely cream-white. This pattern persists over the winter when the upper side of the animal takes on a grey-brown colour.

Plate 2. Welsh Pony with features of wild colouring; note the wide eel-stripe and the dark stripes on the back; the dark stripes on the forelegs do not come out clearly in this picture. (*Photo*: Wiersma).

The pattern is less common among African wild asses. Asiatic wild asses have a predominantly yellow ground colour and a black eel stripe. A dark shoulder cross and zebra stripes on the legs are encountered among African wild asses, of which the Somali sub-species are reddish-grey and the Nubian grizzled-grey, as to ground colour. The various breeds of domestic ass, descended from the African wild ass, of course also display this wild pattern, but in varying strength, to the extent of sometimes differing from the wild ancestor in ground colour. Thus, the great Poitevin ass of Western France, mostly has a dark-brown coat, or even red-bay with light-grey parts under the belly, between the thighs, and round the mouth, eyes and nose. On crossing with the horse (donkey stallion to mare) the pattern is dominantly inherited, so that the mule has a light belly and always the typical nose of an ass. Coat colour is further likewise dependent on the basic colour genes of the horse, so that besides dark-brown and brown-black, dark-grey and yellow-brown coats occur.

Little is as yet known, genetically, about these forms of the wild colour. Probably the pattern in asses and hemiones is caused by another allele, which in its operation is similar to the A^w (white belly agouti) allele in the mouse. Brown horses with a very light belly, ought, according to Odriozola, to carry the A^l (for light) allele. He regards this as the top dominant allele of all the A-series. Thus, it stands above the A^+ allele which is presumed responsible for the wild colour of Przevalsky's Horse.

4:2 COAT COLOUR IN THE FJORD (Vestland) HORSE

[In this section the traditional names given to the various shades of dun will be given in Norwegian (Nynorsk), since exact translations of manageable length do not exist in other languages. But these shades will be exactly defined in English paraphrase. *Tr.*]

From the researches of Loen (1939) and Berge (1963) it is apparent that the colour of the Fjord horse is caused by an allele from the A-series giving a phenotype closely allied to the wild colour. Berge calls it A^D; it produces an almost identical distribution of pigment in the hairs as we described for the Przevalsky Horse. (*See Figure 4[a]*).

Fjord horses are yellow-brown to light-yellow with a somewhat lighter ventral colour. An eel stripe is always present and runs forward as a broad dark band in the centre of the mane, called the *midstol*, and back to the base of the dock. There are often zebra stripes on the legs. The mane has a border of light hairs either side of its black core, known as the *klypping*. There are sometimes inverted V-stripes on the forehead, or a dark patch on the jaw.

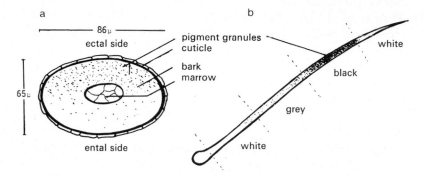

Figure 4. (a) Section of the hair in *brunblakk* Fjord horse. (b) Zonal distribution of pigment in a hair of grå colour.

One, or more, transverse stripes may appear in the mane: they are known as the *grep* [literally "muck fork" – compare Northern English dialect *gripe* with the same meaning. *Tr.*] because of the resemblance to the prongs of a fork. The transverse stripes on the forelegs are situated on the inner and outer sides of the fore-arm, just above the knee: on the hindlegs, less distinctly on the forward edge of the hocks. The colour is that of the eel stripe, only slightly lighter. To this pattern belong also the darker colour of knee, hock, front of cannon bone and pastern. The different shades of colour, or rather varying tints, are related to the presence in the breed of the basic colour genes. Until about 1920, all the usual coat colours found in horses appeared in this breed, but since that time the present almost uniform colour has been very widely propagated, chiefly through the influence of stallions from the lines of Gange Rolf 42 and Njal 166, so that today this colour appears in all Fjord horses. Small white marks are very rare, and not at all popular (Sänger 1962).

Not all the shades that theoretically can occur are in practice easy to distinguish from each other. As from 1922 it has been officially customary to distinguish shades in the following order of frequency: brunblakk, rødblakk, ulsblakk and grå, or muse, while gul and kvit are further recognised (Nordang 1955).

Brunblakk, subdivided into light (lys) and dark (mørk) of which the former is commoner, is the wild form of brown. The coat varies between a dark cream-yellow and a dull pale-brown. The eel stripe is always quite black, as is the dark band in the mane. The klypping is always lighter than the coat. On the flanks, and under the belly, the degree of paleness varies sharply. The head is usually darker than the rest of the body: the colour round the mouth is light. Individual hairs show a clear zonal distribution of pigment: the tip is mostly yellow-brown or grey-brown, the rest yellowish-white. There are also hairs with a white tip and a dark band lower down. The light zone is broadest among the hairs in the groin.

The shading from light to dark may be explained by modifying genes, as in the colours bay and chestnut. But Berge thinks that Fjord horses, which in summer are a very light brunblakk, possess a special factor not belonging to the E-series and seemingly hypostatic, or possibly even intermediary, when crossed with other breeds. The colour of such horses is hardly to be distinguished from ulsblakk, if at all. He presupposes a separate factor h, but cannot make out whether it also influences rødblakk. Possibly it is identical with the factor i, which Salisbury (1941) postulated in order to explain very light chestnut coats. (*See Chapters 5:2 and 6:5*). Thus, this is in opposition to Castle who works exclusively with alleles of the E-series. Berge assumes the presence of the E-allele essential for the occurrence of the brunblakk colour, which can be genetically represented as A^D-B-E. Brunblakk is the most frequent and the most popular colour. The cross brunblakk/brunblakk gives most often brunblakk again, but occasionally also rødblakk.

Rødblakk which was formerly called samblakk is the wild form of chestnut and is sub-divided into light, medium and dark. The

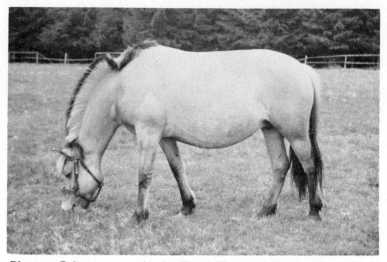

Plate 3. Colour pattern in the Fjord Horse. Stripes on legs clearly visible. Note sharply contrasting band of light hairs along the mane.

coat colour however differs little in tint from that of brunblakk, but the eel stripe is never black, rather light-brown or dark-yellow. The colour round the mouth is light. Rødblakk × rødblakk gives nothing but rødblakk, and it may be written genetically A^D-bbE, or A^Dbbee for the paler shades.

Grå, the wild form of black, light and dark grå are distinguished. The coat varies from a light silver-grey to a dark slate coloured grizzle-grey. The eel stripe is always black. The head is darker than the body, especially round the eyes and mouth and on the ridge of the nose. The "mealy nose" is therefore lacking. *Grå* is highly esteemed but rather rare. It may possibly be compared with the colour of the extinct tarpan. The correct genotypic representation of grå, has not yet been completely clarified because we possess insufficient data on the results of matings between grå and other colours. Grå to grå gives mainly grå, but also rødblakk and kvit. According to Berge the most frequent hairs in the grå coat have a white tip with a black zone below it which shades into grey, the root being white. (*See Figure 4b*). Consequently, there occur in diminishing frequency completely white hairs, grey with a white lower part, and white hairs with a grey band below the tip.

Berge presumes that most grå horses, and certainly those with a darker coat, possess the E^d allele, possibly in homozygote form. It would thus follow that the E^d factor is not totally epistatic vis-à-vis the A^D factor. In rare cases indeed, a grå foal can be born of brunblakk parents. This can hardly be explained, unless one assumes that horses of the ee genotype can likewise be grå. According to Berge the lighter shade, genotypically A^D-B-ee, is involved. Now and then the mating grå × grå gives kvit (the wild form of cream) in which case both parents would carry the dilution gene, the c^{cr} allele (*see Chapter 6:o*). The presence of this gene in heterozygote state is said not to be remarkable in grå. Berge says nothing about the phenotypical colour of the A^D-B-E^d-/eec^{cr}c^{cr}, a grå that is homozygote for the dilution gene. Possibly among the light wild black horses the presence of some which are bearers of the c^{cr} allele, perhaps double (the wild form of mouse-dun, or of pale-dun) is masked. Phenotypically, the wild form of pale-dun could be off-white with barely visible eel stripe, however.

Ulsblakk, once called *lysborket* (light-dun) and light isabella, is known in North Norway as *reinsblakk* or *elgsblakk* (reindeer-dun or elk-dun) and is the colour of the reindeer or the elk at some seasons. It is the wild form of dun and literally means the colour of fresh shorn sheep. The coat is off-white to yellowish-white in colour, the eel stripe is always black. Ulsblakk × ulsblakk can give all shades including kvit. Patently ulsblakk carries the c^{cr} allele, and is thus genetically A^D-B-E-Cc^{cr}. When brunblakk is homozygote for the dilution gene the wild form of perlino occurs, in which the coat is off-white and is only recognizable by the eel stripe, which in such cases is not black but dark-cream to yellow. Ulsblakk is not a popular colour, so that the wild form of perlino occurs rarely.

Gul (yellow) is the wild form of isabella. This colour differs little, if at all, from the ulsblakk, but the eel stripe is never black,

43

but light-bay, as in rødblakk. Genetically it can be written A^D-$bbE/eeCc^{cr}$. Results of mating gul to gul, confirm this view: the result is 50% gul, 25% rødblakk and 25% kvit (Papendieck, 1957).

Kvit (white) is the wild form of cream. The coat is uniformly white and the eel stripe sometimes discernible, from cream to light-yellow in colour. Patently kvit is genetically A^D-$bbE/eec^{cr}c^{cr}$.

Crossing with the ordinary basis colours, the A^D allele behaves dominantly in the inheritance of colour and pattern; the progeny from brunblakk $\times$ bay, however, are often darker than brunblakk and lack the light klypping.

4:3 BAY AND BROWN

As we have already stated, these coats vary in colour from a light sandy-bay to dark-brown and bay-black, by way of reddish-bay and brown shades. Mane and tail and the lower part of the legs are black. In general, the colour comes about by a mixture of black and red hairs, varying over different parts of the body. Sometimes pure black marks are found, for instance a black patch on the croup.

Previous researchers have postulated different theories to explain the bay pattern, either by a separate bay factor assumed (Sturtevant, 1912), (Walther, 1912), or by the presence, understood, of a factor that confines black to the coat of the extremities (Wentworth, 1914), (Crew and Smith, 1930). Nowadays bay is conceived as a special modification of the wild colour (Castle, 1940), (Odriozola, 1951). That is not to say that by now an explanation of all the colours has been found that is genetically viable.

According to the latest authors, the distinction implicit in the traditional English terms must be recognised: a bay group possessing the A allele, and a group having what is called the brown pattern, which is supposed to carry the a^t allele (Castle and Singleton, 1960). But Odriozola differs from Castle in limiting the a^t allele to dark-brown (seal-brown) coats, and sees the other shades as caused by the A^+ allele. He uses the symbol A^L (for light) to indicate the allele for wild colour, while Castle interprets the concept "brown" in a wider sense, understanding thereby all shades of

44

Plate 4. Bay. The coat is near enough uniformly coloured.
The long hairs are black.

the brown pattern. Castle uses the allele A for all bays and browns with a red tint, calling the wild colour A^+. Here it may be further remarked that Castle and his school associate bay with the redder tints of brown. These can be represented in genetic notation as A-B-E for the darker shades and A-B-ee for the lighter tint red-bay. In the case of darker shades (dark-bay) there is very little trace of the red element and the difference from some shades of brown, in terms of hair colour alone, is not always very obvious.

To judge by the cave paintings of palaeolithic Europe which depict horses it is not improbable that brown and bay coats existed in prehistoric times.

Brown is regarded as intermediary between bay and black. Patently the a^t allele is in no position to produce a uniform distribution of eumelanin and pheomelanin throughout the coat. The coat shows what is called the brown pattern with lighter areas round the nose, under the belly (especially to the rear), in the flanks and groin, and, in its most distinct form, between the forelegs and hindlegs,

Plate 5. Light brown with brown pattern, light muzzle and lighter areas on the coat; the long hairs also include light ones. (*Photo*: Wiersma).

behind the elbow and on the rear aspect of the buttocks. The pattern can vary in extent, with all shades, is clearest in light-brown, but seems not to occur with bay. In the darker shades it is only found in the stifle and round the nose, sometimes. The nose can be brown or reddish-brown (coppernose) or even grey-brown to light-grey in breeds such as the Gudbrandsdal (Dølehest of Norway).

The stronger, or weaker, distribution of the light areas may be explained by the e, or the E, allele. Berge thinks that in this case the a^t allele is incompletely epistatic vis-à-vis alleles of the E series, but the idea is rather simplistic. Other shades, such as golden-brown, cannot be explained thus. Apparently special modifying genes are involved. Without going into details, Odriozola assumes series of polygenes for the scale of tints (homomery). Gremmel (1939) thinks that the nature and depth of the colour depend on the quantity, grouping and locality of the pigment granules in the hair: in light-brown, small, evenly distributed granules prevail, while in

46

the darker tints more clusters of the pigment granules occur. Light hairs would also be produced when the pigment is situated more centrally in the bark. Berge points to the zonal pigmentation said also to be present in the hairs of brown coats. In dark-brown he found the following kinds of hair, in order of frequency: wholly black, black with brown tip and grey-white root, brown with white root, and brown with black tip and grey-white root. In the case of light-brown, the commonest hairs were those with a brown tip, black, and completely brown ones. The black mane and tail are not without exceptions, especially with light-brown coat a mixed mane and tail occur now and again (Noriker), and it can also be partially light-brown as, for instance, on the dock, where it is called in some languages the "bloom". Sporadically a wholly light mane and tail occur. (Wriedt, 1928), (Wiersma, 1961).

The dominancy relationship between bay and brown is not yet completely clear. In the view of Castle, the mating bay $\times$ bay can give brown ($a^t aB$) as well as black, because bay can be heterozygote for the alleles A, a^t and a (the genotypes AaB and Aa^{t}B). Conversely, brown $\times$ brown is said to give black, but not bay, since A is dominant over a^t.

This is not consistent with practice. Salisbury (1941) found in the American Shetland Pony that bay $\times$ bay, gave 68·5% bay and 12% brown: bay $\times$ brown gave 50·8% bay and 28·4% brown: brown $\times$ brown, gave 15·3% bay and 51·7% brown.

[Note such statistics could hardly be obtained on the basis of British Shetlands, since the bay colour is so rare in the Islands, that adequate data would scarcely exist, even though the Shetland Stud Book is the earliest founded of British Pony stud books. *Tr.*]

From other stud books, similar data can be drawn, provided one makes allowance for inaccurate entries as regards the distinction between bay-brown and dark-brown and black.

For the statistics given below, the author has drawn on the stud books of the V.L.N. (Gronings type) 1956 and 1957 editions. The colours of 743 progeny have been studied, out of registered mares by black/brown stallions, as well as the colours of the dams. Of the progeny, 2·7% were red-bay. This colour did not seem to be thrown from matings with dark-brown, black/brown, or black mares. There were 5·4% red-bay progeny out of red-bay mares, from brown- or light-brown dams 4·4%, and from mahogany-bay dams 8·5%. Black/brown animals which were produced as 9·4% of the total of mares registered in 1956 and 1957, were mainly thrown by black/brown, dark/brown and black dams, in 47·5%, 24·1% and 20% of the cases respectively. But black/brown also results from the mating of other shades of brown among themselves, or from brown × chestnut. From these data one gets the impression that dark/brown and black/brown, show a consistent dominance over other shades. Berge's experiment with the Dølehest also points to the same conclusion. He thinks that it is more correct to employ the dominant symbol A^t rather than a^t. Moreover, he points to the dominance of the colour pattern in mule breeding. But, as already stated, it is probable that here we have to deal with another allele from the A series. Besides, Berge assumes that A^t allele does not alway dominate the A allele, since obviously mixed forms occur, especially with lighter coats. In this connection it should also be noted that Castle considers horses of the genotype A-B-E^d E can just as easily be black/brown without distinct brown pattern.

TABLE 2

Conspectus of genotypes with dominant A allele
and the relevant phenotypes

Genotype	Phenotype
A^+A^+ BBEE	Wild colour
A^D-B-E^dE^d	grå
A^D-B-E	brunblakk
A^D-B-ee	light grå
A^t-B-E^dE^d	Dominant black (see Chapter 5)
A^t-B-E	Seal brown
A^t-B-ee	brown
A-B-E^dE^d	Dominant black (see Chapter 5)
A-B-E^d	Brown/black (?)
A-B-E	Dark bay
A-B-ee	Red bay

In Table 2 will be found a conspectus of the genotypes discussed and the phenotypes resulting from the combined effect of dominant A alleles, B alleles, and the alleles of the E gene.

From this it appears that the different shades of brown and bay cannot simply be explained without the assumption of a number of modifying genes which possibly have a cumulative effect on colours in the brown/bay group. Castle holds the A and A^t alleles responsible for the occurrence of eel stripe and stripes on the legs with brown coats. Searle considers the possibility that these marks may also be caused by special genes which only affect A genotypes.

The totally recessive mutant of the A series, the a-allele (non-agouti), will be discussed in the next chapter.

CHAPTER 5

THE B-GENE

THE B (for black) factor is held responsible for the formation of melanin pigment, at least according to the most viable interpretations. Only Ordriozola does not postulate a B factor, since, according to him a black coat is caused by the E factor.

It appears from histological (microscopic study of tissue structure) and chemical evidence, that the B locus is concerned with the construction of the protein framework (matrix) of the melanosome (immature pigment granule) and, above all, with its formation of a regular structure. More and more melanin keeps on adhering to it, giving in the end a fully formed homogenous melanin granule. Mutants on this locus give an aberrant shape of granule by structural changes in this matrix, by which colour differences can be explained. It appears further, from skin grafts, that the genes' effect takes place right inside the melanocyte. The B series is not very extensive. The most important mutant is the b (brown) allele which is present in a number of mammals including, among others, the rat, the mouse, the guinea-pig, the rabbit and the dog. It is not yet clear whether this mutant is also present in cattle, with their complicated genetical situation. In the mouse, four alleles are known. Commonly the colour of the eyes is influenced, producing hazel. In bb genotypes, the pigment granules are smaller and spherical in contrast to the oval granules of black (B). The total quantity of eumelanin, in an equal number of granules, is thus smaller. This may explain the brown colour. According to Searle, alleles at the B locus have no effect on the pheomelanin pigment (pheomelanin granules have no regular matrix: the pigment is deposited among a confused mass of fine fibres). Others, such as Jones (1971), think that the C mutant is responsible for a skeleton, or framework, to which pheomelanin alone can adhere.

Just as in B genotypes, in bb genotypes colour variations can also occur through the presence of alleles of the A series. Castle (1961) and Singleton (1969) assume the existence in the horse of the b allele for chestnut, which we shall discuss in connection with black.

5 : 1 BLACK

Just as in rodents, for instance, horses of the genotype aaB are black, and uniformly so, as no pheomelanin is formed. Castle takes genetic differences to account for shades of this colour, as does his school. Ordinary black, which by obliquely falling light in winter can have a rusty gleam, is vulnerable in summer to the bleaching effect of the sun. The coat can then appear black/brown without definite pattern, so that the colour round the mouth mostly stays black. In jet-black, the coat is permanently black with a deep, rather metallic glint. It is found, for instance, in the Shetland pony but also in the Friesian horse. According to Castle (1951), jet-black carries the factor E^d. By assuming this allele, which in its homozygote state is epistatic, vis-à-vis the alleles A and A^t, Castle is able to explain the fact that there is always a varying percentage of brown found in the mating of black $\times$ black. This percentage (8%–13%), is much higher than could be explained by inaccurate descriptions, or by confusion between black and brown/black. Castle also thinks that ee genotypes may be recognised by their phenotype. Odriozola does not postulate a dominant black. He considers black as standing at the end of a series with a more or less fluid transition from brown to black.

Castle's attitude leads to the following conspectus of the different varieties of black:

aaB-E^d-, A-B-E^dE^d, A^t-B-E^dE^d	Dominant black, jet-black.
aaB-E-	Common recessive black; the coat is subject to bleaching, which is also true of the following genotype;
aaB-ee	Black in which the long hairs

are darker than the coat which is rather faded (smoky-black, preto efumaçado) and is best explained as black with black mane and tail.

5:2 CHESTNUT

Even more than bay and brown, the chestnut coat displays a great range of colour shades and tints, ranging from a light yellow-brown and golden-yellow, by way of red tints to dark-brown and black-brown with a russet gleam. The mane and tail are the same colour as the coat, only sometimes a little darker or lighter, or may be of mixed colours, and in some shades more on the grey side, but never black. Even if these are left out of consideration, according to most writers, a chestnut coat can always be recognised as such by the complete absence, even in the darkest shade, of black hairs. Occasionally very dark patches are found in the coat. The difference in tint between summer and winter coat can be very great, especially in ponies.

There are many problems still to be solved about chestnut, and we shall have to touch on several different theories below. Thinking in terms of homology the varieties of colour are most difficult to understand. By contrast, their heredity, not taking account of the graduations of intensity, darkness, etc., is simple: chestnut ✕ chestnut can only give chestnut.

Earlier researchers such as Sturtevant (1912) and Wentworth (1914), but also Odriozola more recently, regard chestnut as a basic colour in which the B gene is inactive whereas Castle and his collaborators see chestnut genetically as bb (understanding b as the recessive allele of the B gene). In that case the different tints and notably the typical red one would depend on modifying genes, whether or not in collaboration with alleles of A and E series (Singleton and Bond 1966, Singleton 1969).

As with brown it is improbable that the different shades of chestnut, can be exclusively explained by alleles of the E series. It is much more probable that a number of polygenes are to be assumed which are not, as Merkens (1953) thinks, homomers of the C (for colour) gene. Up to now, despite the labours of Wentworth, McCann (1916), Wright (1917), Gremmel (1939) and Salisbury (1931), no one has succeeded in finding any logical progression in the inheritance of the shades. But all found that sorrel is recessive vis-à-vis chestnut. That is, taking sorrel as not just the light yellow-brown coats, but also the light red shades, whereas chestnut is the deeper and redder colour.

Castle and Singleton (1961), and after that Singleton and Bond (1966), produced a rather simple seeming hypothesis for at least some phenotypical variations. This takes account of the A- and E-factors, and opposes two groups with the relationship of black to brown. The A factor causes an aberrant colour in the long hairs (usually lighter than the coat) while the E factor makes the coat darker but has no influence on the mane etc.

Plate 6. Light chestnut, flaxen mane, rather light under belly.

(*Photo*: Wiersma)

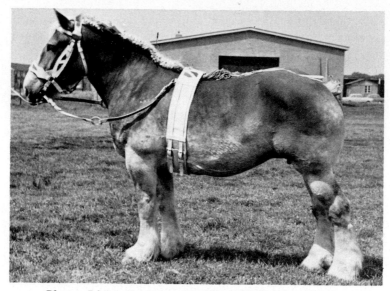

Plate 7. Light chestnut, with diffuse light region of coat.
(*Photo*: Royal Netherlands Draught Horse Association)

Group I includes the genotypes:

aabbE-   Liver-chestnut (uniformly coloured).
aabbee   Sorrel (uniformly coloured).

Group II includes chestnuts with the A factor, which thus, mated to black, can throw brown foals:

A-bbE-   Chestnut, with mane and tail lighter than the coat, but still of the same tint.
A-bbee   Light chestnut (sorrel) with a coat that is darker than the mane and tail.

Neither Castle nor Singleton have clearly explained why the mane and tail in A-chestnuts differ from the coat. They assume that the brown b-pigment is always concentrated by the A factor in the long guard hairs and so gives an optically lighter effect than in the hairs of the coat in which it occurs moreover in conjunction with pheomelanin. There are no ideas as yet about the phenotype of chestnuts which carry the allele E^d. Apparently it is dark chestnuts which can carry the A factor invisibly.

The above hypothesis, which relies chiefly on the findings of palomino breeding (*see Chapter 6*) is not universally accepted. Thus, Berge's opinion is that one cannot tell by looking at a chestnut coat whether the A factor is present. He says further, that it is more logical to assume, by analogy with brown, that the ee genotypes have mane and tail somewhat darker (red) than the coat. In fact, this does happen. Jones, who, incidentally, has a quite different conception of the workings of the E alleles, thinks there are indications favouring the thesis that the A allele has the effect of making the coat lighter in colour, just as it does with brown.

And therefore, he calls all A-bb genotypes sorrel. The e allele, according to him, has no visible effect. And the E allele restricts the full distribution of eumelanin, as well of pheomelanin, both before and after the A factor has influenced coat colour.

Of a third group of chestnuts, genotype A^t-bb, it is not yet possible to say how the coat will look; according to Castle, like a chestnut with brown pattern, while Singleton and Bond admit the possibility that this is the genotype of the claybank colour, a dull yellowish-brown, or brownish-red with mane and tail the same hue or a little darker. It often also has an eel stripe.

Besides the phenotypes discussed one comes across chestnuts with a very light cream, or flaxen, mane that is clearly different from the mane of A-chestnuts. But one has the impression that in manes of this sort there are gradual transitions into lightness.

The question of very light manes, as a separate characteristic, has much occupied previous researchers. Wentworth assumes, from his researches on the American-Belgian Draught horse, in which the prevailing colour is a light chestnut with flaxen mane, a simple recessive heredity dependent on the pair of factors ff (for flaxen). McCann's experiments on the same breed are more comprehensive but less conclusive. He considers sorrel a separate colour, which is recessive in respect of all other colours. He established that sorrel

X sorrel gave only sorrel offspring and that sorrel X black in most cases gave sorrel and bay, and, less frequently, chestnut and black. Although he gives no genotype for this sorrel, his results support the theory of Castle, that sorrel = A-chestnut.

Salisbury believes that the heredity is more complicated than that. Chestnut, with light mane, was found in 25% of offspring of ordinary chestnuts and in 90% of progeny of chestnut parents with light manes, in the American Shetland pony. In the Finnish horse, he found light mane with ordinary chestnut in 32·6%, with sorrel in 30·3%, and with dark-chestnut or liver-chestnut in 9·6% of cases. Liver-chestnuts came chiefly from liver-chestnut parents, and least often from sorrel parents. Salisbury considers liver-chestnut dominant over ordinary chestnut, with a tendency to intermediary heredity, and supposes an I (intensive) factor. The light mane in liver-chestnut must indicate recessivity, and possibly two pairs of genes come into play.

On this rather complicated material, the following is to be noted.

In chestnut the coat not only shows great variability in the degree of lightness, but so also does that of the mane, at least when it is of a different colour from the coat. Although the light coloured mane is to a consistent degree independent of the coat colour (Merkens, 1953), it still occurs most frequently with the light shades. Sometimes it is part coloured, and occasionally combinations, such as light mane and dark tail may be found. Salisbury postulates that the f-gene exerts a consistent influence on the depth of the coat colour, whereas its expression can be variable as regards the mane. Moreover, in light chestnuts with light mane such as occur in pony breeds (but also in heavy horses of the Belgian type), the coat appears to have a certain pattern of light areas under the belly, behind the elbow, round the pastern and fetlock. This is most obvious in the winter coat. The lighter the coat, the more extensive this light ventral region is. Often there is also dappling. This is very often found in the Haflinger, even in the summer coat. Most Haflingers have very light, flaxen or almost white manes and tails. After that, light-grey or silver-grey manes seem commonest, as in alézan brulé, and a more part coloured mane with the medium and dark-chestnut coats. In such cases the darkest hairs come in the middle of the mane and tail. It is possible that the A-bb chestnuts mentioned by Castle are of this pattern, the shading of coat colour, but above all the distribution of light areas, being influenced by modifying genes, as in brown. By contrast, the opinion of others, such as Jones (1971), is that a very light mane is a recessive feature, dependent on one, or several, pairs of genes.

An eel stripe sometimes occurs in the Haflinger. Castle ascribes this, as well as the brown pattern, to the effect of the A gene. But it is possible that this feature is due to an independent property which is dominantly inherited. This in view of the fact that an eel stripe only occurs in certain families, having no connection with the colour of the coat.

CHAPTER 6

THE DILUTION GENES

GENES WHICH so influence the coat colour, that to the eye the colour looks weaker, so that brown becomes beige, and black blue-grey, are called dilution genes. The two most important series of multiple alleles of this group, occurring in most mammalian species are called C (for colour) and D (for dilution).

The C gene, of which the totally recessive mutant is also called the albino factor, is held responsible for the occurrence of complete colour by facilitating the production of eumelanin and pheomelanin out of its components with full intensity. The symbol C is mostly omitted in genetic formulae, since the C gene is always present in coloured individuals.

Recessive C alleles, acting directly on the melanocyte, function, in general, with a gradual reduction of pigmentation by diminuition of the number of granules. This happens first to the pheomelanin granules, and later on to the eumelanin granules. In the latter, there is also a change in their size and shape. The best known of the allelo-morph series, in the c^{ch} allele, occurring in rodents, cats, and possibly also dogs. It gives what is called the chinchilla pattern to an agouti coat. This pattern arises from total suppression of pheome-lanin and retention of eumelanin. C alleles in mice can be arranged in a series with steadily stronger diluting action until at last no more pigment is formed due to complete suppression of tyrosinatic activity. One can then speak of authentic albinos, with no pigment in hair, skin or eyes (genotype cc).

Recessive mutants of the D gene also act to dilute colour, but by way of a quite different mechanism. Lumps are formed, both of eumelanin and pheomelanin granules, and the equitable distribution of pigment is thus disturbed. So light absorption diminishes. By this effect, for instance, black is "watered down" to blue-grey. In mice, which show four D alleles, a second characteristic is the abnormal nucleopetal melanocytes (those in which pigment granules are located, not in the long processes of the cell, but round the core of the cell).

In other species, such as dogs and cats, there is as far as we know but one mutant, known as d allele. The occurrence of this homologous allele, as in other colour factors, is assumed on grounds of homologous effect, but is sometimes less justified – and dubious – where the most important characteristic – the clumping of granules – is missing, as in the rabbit. In this animal colour dilution occurs through an absence of pigment granules in the bark of the hair.

In the horse also it has not yet been possible to determine by what gene dilute colours are caused. Nevertheless, a dilution gene does occur in almost all breeds of horse and pony.

Horses whose coat looks dilute, washy, watered down, or pale, have from ancient times been known among Oriental and Asiatic breeds. This special colour has, in time past, spread all over Europe; possibly by way of Spain. But in modern times, it only occurs sporadically in light horse breeds (as opposed to ponies) though it is widely distributed among the horse stock of America. In Holland dilute colour in recent years has again proliferated by the influence of the stallion Rheinfeld 199, imported in 1941 from Oldenburg.

Previous researchers, among them Wilson (1912), had as yet no clear insight into the genetic structure of dilute colour. Walther (1912) and Ströver (1917) took it to be yet another basic colour caused by dominant ground pigment. Wentworth (1914) assumed a dilution factor I, and Wright (1917) a factor D, while Gremmel (1939) in his histological experiments found no connection between isabella on the one hand and dun, and mouse-dun, on the other. A better insight into the genesis of these colours is due to the research of Salisbury and Castle, which showed that Wright's view was correct, and which also proceeded from the basis of the D factor.

The effect of this factor may be seen as incompletely dominant, or intermediary, in the sense that the hair colour in homozygote form is more dilute than in heterozygote types. The exact effect of this gene is, however, still not quite clear. According to Gremmel, the pigment granules are mainly concentrated on one side of the hair, at least in dun, which causes an alteration in light absorption.

Odriozola assumes that the dilution gene is an allele of theC-series represented as c^{cr} (for cream), without dominance but intermediary in outward effect. He supposes it attacks eumelanin less strongly than pheomelanin. This on the strength of the fact that it corresponds more closely to the C alleles in rodents, and because the postulated D gene (partially dominant) is an exception to the rule that only recessive mutants occur in other species. Furthermore, in the light of the dominant D gene, recessive alleles are to be expected in the horse too, though they have not yet been found. On the basis of these arguments, Singleton and Bond (1966) also prefer to use the symbol c^{cr} in place of the symbol D. Odriozola's hypothesis cannot however be proved by tests on allelomorphy because genuine albinism (cc) does not occur in the horse.

The possibility is therefore not to be excluded, that in the horse we have to reckon with a quite specific gene, the more so since arguments in favour of Castle and Singleton's ideas can be adduced from the data of palomino breeding. They establish that the effect of the dilution gene is only visible in genotypes carrying the A allele. This view was already advanced by Domanski and Prawochenski (1948) from indications of results produced at the Russian State Stud at Enisherlov. They noticed that, from the mating of isabella with black brown and dun foals were also produced. This point is still partly a debated question, as we shall see below.

It may be noted that in cattle, a dominant dilution gene occurs with effects analogous to those in the horse. This gene in the heterozygote state dilutes black to dark dun and in the homozygote state to pale dun (Hagedorn, 1934), (Barkema, 1970). Colours that arise from the effect of the c^{cr} factor on brown, black and chestnut will now be discussed in detail.

6:1 DUN

In the dilute brown, or dun, coat the colour is indifferently light-brown, or yellow-brown, while the mane and tail and the lower part of the legs remain black. Sometimes the mane may include

Plate 8. Dun, yellow-brown coat and black mane. (*Photo*: Wiersma).

pale-brown hairs, or be a rather greyish-black; sometimes there is a black rim round the ears.

This coat colour was formerly often confused with the wild colour. Tuff (1933) still thought there was some connection with the colour of the Fjord horse.

This confusion is understandable, since an eel stripe is often found in dun horses, and the winter coat in ponies especially, gives a "wild" impression due to the occurrence of light and dark parts (as on the forehand and the shoulder). Generally the head is also somewhat darker than the coat, round the eyes and on the cheeks, while the ridge of the nose is lighter. Moreover there is a distinct zonal distribution of pigment in the hair.

The author found in the coat of a dark-dun pony besides black and yellow hairs with black tip, yellow hairs with white tip and grey-black base, yellow hairs with grey base, and a small number of strongly diluted pale coloured hairs which in oblique light gave a silvery effect. The winter coat of this pony was much lighter, and

Plate 9. Perlino, or silver-dun. The mane is not white but still shows some contrast with the coat. (*Photo*: Wiersma).

more of a beige colour on the body, because the long hairs had a broad yellow zone below the dark tip, while the base was grey or light-grey. According to Castle, this is not the effect of the working of the c^{cr} allele, but an expression of the A genotype, normally invisible, or barely visible. But it does become clearly visible through the c^{cr} factor, which does not work, or works less strongly in places where the eumelanin is concentrated. In the light yellow-dun colour typical of the Highland pony, the coat hairs, except for a greyish-black base, are all yellow. Sometimes these ponies have a light-grey muzzle, and often, besides an eel stripe, dark stripes on the legs and a broad band over the withers, the edges of which are blurred ("shadow").

Genetically, dun is written $A-B-Cc^{cr}$. Presence of the E factor makes the coat dark with a dull yellow-brown tinge that can be confused with light-bay. The ee genotype would have a bright yellow to yellowish-bay coat, a colour that is called buckskin in the United States to distinguish it from dun of other shades. According to Castle's hypothesis, the effect of the c^{cr} allele on brown (genotype A^t-B) would not be visible, nor would it be so on blacks of the genotype A-B-E^dE^d. According to Singleton and Jones, A^t-B horses would be dun.

When the dilution gene is present in homozygote form, in bays (genotype A-B-$c^{cr}c^{cr}$) the result is a colour called perlino or silver dun. In this, the coat is dark-cream to off-white, with a mane always clearly darker than the coat, but about the same tint. Clearly the eumelanin is now being attacked. Since the pigment too, in the first layers of the iris (the stroma) is strongly dilute, perlinos like other $c^{cr}c^{cr}$ genotypes have blue eyes. Blue eyes arise as the result of dispersion of light through small bodies (what is called the Tyndall effect) against a dark background, in this case, the rear part of the iris which contains much pigment. Nothing can yet be said with certainty about the colours that would be produced in the genotypes A^t-B-$c^{cr}c^{cr}$ and A-B-$c^{cr}c^{cr}E^dE^d$, but it is reasonable to think that here too colour variations would arise.

6:2 MOUSE-DUN

The mouse-dun colour caused by the effect of the dilution gene on black is difficult to describe and hard to distinguish in some cases. The coat can appear mouse-grey to ashen, but also in oblique lights can look reddish-brown, so that one finds mouse-dun registered as brown/black, faded-black or very dark-dun. Mane and tail are black, but sometimes rusty-black. The ideal mouse-dun colour has a grey-blue glint.

Castleton and Singleton leave no place in their scheme for mouse-dun, since they assume that the dilution gene has no visible effect on the aaB genotype. But this is clearly in contradiction to practice. Mouse-dun offspring of dun parents, for instance, do occur, but it is also a fact that mouse-dun as such is often scarcely or not at all to be recognised by the coat colour. The most striking example is the stallion Rheinfeld himself (genotype aaBbCc^{cr}) who is down in the book as black. That is also the case with many of his daughters, who cannot be distinguished from ordinary black but, on account of their offspring, may well be genetically mouse-dun; probably these horses carried the E^d allele. Rheinfeld left mouse-dun foals,

Plate 10. The yellow eye (called "goat's eye") of the mouse-dun
stallion Rheinfeld (*Photo*: Wiersma).

both out of brown and brown-black and black mares, which from the
point of view of their pedigree are genetically aaBb or aaBB.
There can thus be no support for the hypothesis of Castle's, that the
genotype aaB-Cc^{cr} is not mouse-dun, but common black. The different tints of mouse-dun possibly depend on modifying genes that
have no visible effect on the normal black coat. According to some,
the true mouse-dun colour occurs in E genotypes, while the ee-
genotype gives a tendency to more of a light-grey tint with black
mane, such as is called in Latin America *grullo*. According to Jones
(1971), it is a more faded brown coat (grullo brown) that is the
phenotype when the A^{t} allele is present.

Although Singleton does not expand on the effect of the dilution gene in homozygote form on black, it is generally considered
that coat colour in what is called pale-dun is similar to perlino, and
is thus off-cream with slightly darker mane. Possibly the coat in its
darker shades is very light-grey-brown, to grey-yellow. Within fore-

64

seeable time, more exact data are to be expected on this point, since under Singleton's direction breeding experiments are being carried out at the moment at the Colonial Farm of the University of Virginia.

6:3 ISABELLA

The dilute chestnut colour is called isabella. In general, the coat shows a variety of tints, ranging from a light, bright, or dull-yellow, to a dark-brown-yellow, sometimes appearing rather grey-brown, so that dark-isabella is sometimes erroneously registered as greyish-chestnut. The mane is flaxen to silvery-white. The darker shades, often dappled, are thus similar to drab chestnut but with a much lighter and more uniformly coloured mane, which may be ascribed to the E factor.

Palomino foals, like dun foals, at birth are mostly light-cream. The dilution gene in homozygote form, makes the coat very light: from light-cream to off-white. The mane is white and the eyes blue. This is called cremello, or blue-eyed-cream. Sometimes, cremellos have what are called glass eyes, or wall eyes, that is the iris is greyish-blue to marbled-white. In that case, we are dealing with a very dense stroma to the iris, which reflects nearly all the light.

The designation "isabella" is becoming obsolete and is more and more being supplanted by "palomino". But palomino in the strict sense is properly the name of the special golden shade of isabella, a popular colour, above all in the United States, where it is extensively bred. The palomino coat varies from a bright-cream like golden-yellow, via brazen to a rather dull light-gold brown-yellow. The ideal shade is described as the colour of a newly minted gold coin, but this variation is excessively rare (Norton, 1949). The colour is sensitive to the bleaching effect of sunlight, and becomes even paler in winter. Mane and tail are supposed to be white or ivory coloured. According to Harrero (1945) there are very dark palominos with a dark-brown coat that has a perceptible golden glint and a white mane. Very light palominos are called palomillo. According to Castle, the ideal tint only occurs in individuals of the ee genotypes, and further, still unknown modifying genes are assumed to exist. In the palomino, eyes and skin may be normally coloured (dark), but also lighter (hazel eyes).

Salisbury and Britton (1941), Castle and King (1951) and Singleton and Bond (1966) who have done extensive research on this colour, came to the conclusion that palomino (i.e. isabella) can only occur in chestnuts with an A factor. On wholly recessive chestnuts of the genotype aabb, the effect of the dilution gene may not be visible. It is not obvious at once, and the animal may be mistaken for an ordinary chestnut. These are what Castle called crypto-palominos, meaning presumably that the coat may be somewhat lighter but in every case uniformly chestnut throughout. Indeed, it has already been noted that palominos can be born of two chestnut parents, of whom one obviously was an unseen carrier of the dilution factor. We have here a situation analogous to that in mouse-dun.

Plate 11. Isabella, or palomino. The coat is slightly dappled, the mane white. (*Photo:* Wiersma).

As regards isabella, practice has so far not been reconciled with theory. The stallion Rheinfeld in every foaling season has always begotten isabellas, not only out of brown and chestnut mares, but also out of black ones. Isabella out of a black mare can in this case hardly have a genotype other than aabbCc^{cr}, unless the black parent was genotypically A-BbE^{d}E^d, which does not happen very often.

It is further remarkable that Rheinfeld had yellow-brown eyes, which are known as hazel, as a consequence of a dilute pigmentation in the stroma of the iris. This feature which can be traced back to the third generation in his pedigree (Wiersma, 1955) occurs in many of his progeny, not only in isabellas and duns, but also in the mouse-dun (Homan, 1952). In view of this characteristic, and the occurrence of mouse-dun, it is according to Berge, not wholly impossible that in Rheinfeld we have a case of another allele of the dilution gene. Hazel eyes seem to occur with palominos in other ways too. It is not yet clear why the colour of the iris should be diluted in one instance, and not in another. In other species, the D alleles as well as the C alleles cause dilution of colour in the iris.

As yet, no satisfactory answer can be given to the question why the mane of the palomino is white. Castle at first assumed that the bb-eumelanin was more strongly attacked than was pheomelanin by the dilution factor. Singleton admitted that he had not so far found a valid explanation for this phenomenon. But it is possible there is some connection with a special structure of the hairs in the mane. Possibly also, the pigment granules in these hairs were differently distributed already before, or just after, the effect of the dilution gene, whereby optically a very light aspect would be obtained.

Uncertainty persists still about the genotype of the claybank-dun colour, which is also called red-dun, which is a lighter tint than claybank *tout simple*. The coat is uniformly a ruddy-yellow. Sometimes the mane can be rather darker than the coat. Odriozola counts this colour as a special variety of dilute chestnut, but without going into the genotypical picture. According to Castle the genotype would be A^t–bbCc^{cr}, a view that Singleton does not share.

If the above theory concerning palomino is correct, then it fol-

Plate 12. Cremello. In contrast to perlino the coat here is uniformly cream. (*Photo*: Wiersma).

lows in practice that palomino X palomino is the safest way to breed palominos. Two palomino parents have a 37·5% to 50% chance at most, of getting a palomino foal if one is A-bbCc^{cr} and the other AAbb. The most successful mating is that of cremello A-bbc^{cr}c^{cr}X A-chestnut. From this 75% and even 100% palomino foals can ensue, if one of the parents is homozygote for the A allele. Even the mating of cremello with brown, which ·is heterozygote for the B allele (AaBb or AABb) gives palomino, with a chance between 37·5% and 50%. The chances in the case of palomino X brown of course are only half as great. The only uncertain element in matings of the last two sorts mentioned is the Bb condition of the brown parent, unless it is known from the pedigree. Finally, palominos can be born from the mating dun X brown, black or chestnut and from mouse-dun X brown or chestnut.

68

A particular colour shade, with dilute characteristics, known as silver dappled, or *prateado rodado*, is found in the American Shetland Pony. It is also called dappled chestnut because of its colour relationship with chestnut. It was first remarked in 1897 in the stallion, Chestnut 3572. But so far as can be ascertained, the colour, which is undoubtedly a mutation, first occurred without doubt in the mare, Trot 31, who was born in 1886. She is described as "fawn", dappled, with a white mane and tail. Her daughter, Keitberger 1752, dark-cream with white mane but no dapples, threw to the deep-black stallion Prince of Wales, the colt, Chestnut. The latter is regarded as the foundation sire of all silver dappled ponies now extant.

The colour is not a variation of chestnut, but arises by the effect of a dominant gene, which so dilutes black and brown pigment that the coat becomes chestnut; the tint varies from very dark-cream with a silvery sheen to light chocolate-beige, while the mane is always white or silver. Castle and Smith (1953), give a description of the colour and its genetic background. They found that the E, or E^d, alleles are requisite for the typical dappling of the coat (alternate light and dark hairs in the form of dapples, as in dappled grey). It appears further, that the A-gene must be present to produce the white, clearly contrasting mane and tail.

On grounds which are not entirely clear, Castle postulated the symbol S (for silvery) for this dilution gene, because the coat included strongly dilute white and silver-grey hairs. But this symbol has long been used for the S series (for self = whole colour), of which the recessive mutants produce piebald. Also, this colour has no connection with those which are caused by the Si (for silvering) gene. On grounds of the relationship between the effects of D gene (c^{cr} allele), Berge (1963) prefers to use D^s, although no tests on allelomorphy are known. For want of better, we shall use this last named symbol. It is not clear if homologies to the D^s gene exist in other species.

The D^s factor is almost completely dominant. Homozygotes are hardly any lighter in colour. As in breeding for this special colour, use is principally made of the mating of silver dappled chestnut with deep-black, or silver dappled chestnut with silver dappled chestnut, there are insufficient data about the phenotype resulting from all theoretically possible genotypes. In some phenotypes, it is also a question whether a satisfactory distinction can be made. This is particularly true of aa genotypes.

The following variations can be listed:

A-B-E^d-/E-D^s	Dark, dappled chestnut, dappled silver, white mane, the most desired colour; the E genotype is called medium dark.
A-B-eeD^s	The coat is the same as sorrel, or light chestnut, without dapples, the mane being white; very like palomino and subject to confusion with it.
A-bbE^d-/E-D^s	Light dappled chestnut; a conspicuously lighter coat, the inside of the dapples almost cream.
A-bbeeD^s	Very light chestnut coat (?) with white mane; no dapples.
aaB-E^d-/E-D^s-	Dappled chestnut, with little or no contrast between mane and coat.
aaB-eeD^s-	Uniform chestnut or sorrel (?)
aabbE^d-/E-/eeD^s	Uniform sorrel (?)

The D^s gene shows a certain interaction with the G factor, so that a new variant of white-born-white, grey-white, results. It has been seen that the simultaneous occurrence of D^s and G factors leads to the accelerated occurrence of a strong grey colour, often present at birth, especially in -B-E^d/E genotypes, so that the foals go white very quickly.

In silver dappled chestnut, light eyes sometimes occur, hazel but also blue. According to Castle, this is a hall-mark of bb genotypes.

6:5 OTHER DILUTION GENES

Berge thinks there may be other dilution genes, in view of the many varieties of dilute colour, such as are found in Latin America. He is, therefore, unwilling to reject Wentworth's postulated I (for intensive) factor without further ado. The mutant allele, i, could be responsible for the very pale varieties of chestnut and brown already discussed under chestnut. The inheritance is not totally recessive, but, according to Berge, seems more intermediary, possibly in relation to the A factor, bearing in mind the pattern in which lighter areas mostly occur in these chestnuts.

CHAPTER 7

GREY GENES, ROAN GENES

IT IS characteristic of the grey coat, that it is made up of hairs that have no pigment and thus give the impression of being white. Experiments on rodents, and with artificial forms of white hair caused by X-rays and freeze-branding (with the branding iron cooled in liquid nitrogen) show that the process of pigment loss takes place at the level of the hair follicules, through the absence, or gradual loss of, mature and active melanocytes from the follicle, so that no pigment granules get into the hair.

In the horse, at least two forms of grey colouring are to be distinguished, each caused by a separate gene.

7:1 VARIABLE GREY

For this form of progressive, or bleaching, grey the G (for grey) factor is accounted responsible. Homologues of this gene are found in rabbits, mice, rats and guinea pigs, rather in the recessive form (si gene). Also in dogs and in some breeds of sheep. The phenotypic effect varies from species to species, and also depends on the presence of other colour factors.

In the horse, the G factor is totally dominant, so that externally there is no difference between heterozygote and homozygote greys. Well known homozygote greys were, *inter alia,* the Dutch stallion Tello 137 DPS and the Hanoverian Aṁhurath III. Horses with the G factor are born, not grey, but in the basic colour, although sometime at birth there are a few white hairs round the eyes and in the ears.

The greying process is often visible at the first change of coat, and continues from then onwards, so that after five to ten years the horse is white all over, but the skin and eyes stay dark. It is not yet

Plate 13. Grey. The coat is slightly dappled, but in the course of years will turn white all over.

clear what the variation in greying time depends on. According to Salisbury, homozygote greys go white quicker: in the Welsh pony it is observed that foals of grey parents after shedding the foal coat are already a pronounced grey.

In old grey horses that have turned white one may sometimes observe the occurrence of pigmented hairs in the form of little spots ("fleabitten"). This is the result of re-activation of surviving melanocytes. As a possible pleiotropic effect of the G gene one can regard the formation of melanomata (tumours of dark pigment "moles") in the skin, especially in the perianal region (pleiotropy of colour factors in the horse occurs seldom, or has not yet been discovered, but is not uncommon in other species).

Dappling, that is patches of a stronger degree of grey colour, has been discussed in G-greys by Sturtevant, Wentworth, and Wriedt; Wentworth assumed a special factor (D), that would be epistatic to the G gene. According to Gremmel and Züblin (1947) the dappled appearance is simply a stage in the progressive greying process and is not dependent on any genetic factor. Dapples also occur, apart from grey colour, in bay, brown, chestnut and even black coats.

It is then often ascribed to a good state of nutrition. From Züblin's researches the following conclusions emerge:

(a)   The dapples (spots where there are more white hairs than elsewhere) seem to be centres of networks of capillary arteries. The degree of pigmentation depends on the blood supply. But there is no connection with subcutaneous layers of fat.
(b)   The skin under a dapple also appears less pigmented than its surroundings.
(c)   The hairs in a dapple are shorter than those outside it.
(d)   Dappling is a temporary stage in star shaped progressive depigmentation of hairs, and (less so) of epidermis proceeding from many centres.

7:2 PERMANENT OR INVARIABLE GREY (ROAN)

This form is caused by the R (for roan) factor; which is also regarded as completely dominant, though there are some indications of partial dominance.

Whether homologues exist in other species is doubtful, and will remain so as long as we have no clear insight into the effect of the R gene.

In mice, an incompletely dominant Rn gene is known, and in the karakul breed of sheep an R factor exists that is lethal when homozygote.

Some see in dogs a relationship between the R factor, and the T (for ticking) factor.

In cattle the situation is still more complicated, though Ibsen (1933) assumed a recessive w gene, with an effect like roan. The recessive r gene postulated by Smith (1925) or Ibsen's N factor in cattle probably does not belong to the roaning factors.

There are phenotypical differences in the horse in the degree of roaning; together with a moderately strong effect it is observed that in the Dutch Draught horse many R greys (possibly homozygote) are strongly roaned and so are very light in colour. The white hairs in the coat are evenly distributed: dappling never occurs. The extremities of the legs, the head and mane, are not affected, or only in a slight degree: mane and tail then comprise a varying quantity of grey white, or white, hairs. Roan is apparent at the first change of coat in the foal, and changes but little through life.

Castle's old idea, recently reproduced by Searle once more, that the R factor in homozygote condition would be lethal, has long been refuted in practice. In the Belgian (Ardennais) Draught horse, many examples of RR horses occurred in the past, and in Holland of recent years the Draught stallions Quarre K.2404 and Costaud de Marche K.2322 are well known, both being homozygote roans, the

Plate 14. Roan.

75

former on black, the latter on bay. Through these two sires and through an increasing use of bay roan stallions in general (from 20·6% in 1954 to 70% in 1964) there has been a great expansion of the roan colour; whereas in 1954 only 36% of foals were roan (25·2% of these being bay roan), in 1964 this percentage had risen to 64·6% and of these 47·8% were bay roan.

7:3 TICKED WITH WHITE HAIRS

In ticking too, white hairs are found scattered throughout the coat. Sometimes they are more frequent in particular areas, such as the flanks, but never so as to give the appearance of a roan horse. Ticking would be apparent at the first change of coat, after which there would be no change in its intensity. It occurs in light as well as heavy horses, but in sharply varying percentages. It is very general in the Dutch Light Horse, in the Noriker and the Haflinger. But it can also die out utterly, as in the Friesian horse, in which it once occurred in 2·5% of individuals.

In the Dutch Draught breed some years ago, before roan became the prevailing colour, 25% of individuals were ticked with white. Fashions change.

Genetically little is yet known about ticking. Walther (1913), assumed a non-dominant factor with "transgressive fluctuating expression." Merkens (1953), rather suspected an allele of the R series, and presented a graduation from light ticking to light roan to pronounced roan as RR, RŔ, and Ř Ŕ. Indeed ticking is closely allied to roan, and the progeny of roan horses can be ticked.

Berge postulates a separate dominant gene on grounds of the observation that the Gudbrandsdal stallion Borgen 1416 bequeathed his ticked coat dominantly. This idea finds support in the researches of Wolning and de Groot (1935). They found among a total of 537 progeny by ticked stallions (Dutch Draught) that there were 48% ticked individuals. All the stallions begat ticked and whole coloured foals. These data mean that an unifactorial dominant inheritance is likely. Among the foals were also 48 roans, of which 7 were out of non-roan dams. This total is rather large to be caused solely by incorrect registration and suggests that there may be a connection between roan and ticked coats.

76

It would be well to examine whether any relationship exists between ordinary ticked coats and roan (R) and the form of roan in spotted horses and piebalds of the Sabino type (*see Chapter 8*).

As regards the dominance relationship between the G and the R factors, Odriozola supposes that they are mutations independent of one another, whereby it is assumed at present that the G factor is epistatic to the R factor. A horse born roan will later turn white if it possesses the G factor. And both factors are epistatic vis-à-vis the c^{cr} allele.

CHAPTER 8

THE SPOTTING GENES

PARTICOLOURED COATS occur in practically all mammalian species. But, here again, it is among the rodents that the white spotting genes have been most widely investigated. Thus, in mice, at least seven factors are known to cause white spots. Here we shall confine ourselves to the W and S genes, as the most commonly occurring homologous important factors.

According to Searle (1968), apart from mice, one finds homologues of the S gene (for self = whole-colour) in golden hamsters, guinea-pigs, rabbits, mink, cats, dogs and cattle. Alleles of this series produce generally white patches, irregular, mainly on the ventral parts of the coat and the extremities. The rest of the coat can, as in the cavy (guinea-pig), look grey or roan. Piebaldness shows a clearly quantitative picture, since the expression is very much subject to the effect of gene modification. This is true to such an extent that it is easy to select for extreme forms, such as a whole white coat or a given pattern of piebald. Expansion of white also happens through interaction with other spotting genes or by additive effects in homomery. Most S alleles are recessive, except in cats and mink. In dogs, where incompletely recessive forms are known, the s^w allele when homozygote causes an all white coat.

The W (for white) series consists mainly of dominant alleles, leading to intermediary forms of expression. The heterozygotes are piebald; sometimes linked with dilution of pigment in the coloured hairs: the homozygotes are in most animals all white, often showing serious defects in different organs and are at times not capable of life (viable). Even among W alleles there is a tendency to interaction generally, in the sense of an increase in white patches, with other spotting genes, so that, for example, W + s gives an all white coat.

Homologues to the W gene are found in hamsters, cats and foxes.

The point of attack by the piebald gene is the formation and migration of the melanoblast, but an effect is also possible through the cellular environment, operating on the proliferation of the peripheral melanoblast and/or the invasion by the melanoblasts of the hair follicles and their ripening there into the melanocytes. It is clear that where the migration of the melanoblasts is hindered, the unpigmented areas will occur in places lying farthest from the neural crest, hence at the extremities and the ventral aspect of the trunk. If not all the follicles contain melanocytes a grey roan appearance will occur by diffuse attack.

It is obvious that most researchers in different forms of pied have been thinking alike (in the case of the horse) about alleles of the W and S series. Here again, the establishment of homologues meets with difficulties as in the horse there are no pleiotropic perceptible effects of these genes which are the rule among other species, barring some exceptions. White spotting in the horse is indeed still most incompletely investigated, so that in the description of the different phenotypic varieties the genetic concept is defective, or is provisionally totally wanting.

We shall not expiate here on the factors that cause a regular piebald pattern in many wild species: they too have been little investigated as yet, and probably have no homologues in the horse.

8:1 PIEBALD AND SKEWBALD

This is a frequently recurring form of dominant spotting, the common picture being a basic coat colour with mostly very large and sharply defined white areas, irregularly distributed over the body. Although all parts of the body can be white, one gets the impression that white areas occur more often on the neck, shoulder, ribs, back and croup than on the breast, belly, flanks and head. Often the normal white markings on the head and legs are larger in piebald than in non-pied horses.

This colour is very widespread among light horses in America. In Europe it was traditional in the Dutch Light horse. It is also found among some pony breeds, such as the Shetland [the only British native pony breed whose stud book does not debar piebalds from registration. *Tr.*] and the Icelander.

Phenotypically, piebald and skewbald show very great variations. Extreme forms occur, among others, in what Americans call the Morocco Spotted Horse, and in the Shetland pony. The Morocco usually has a wholly white body and legs, while the head and part of the neck are wholly coloured. Possibly this is a form that has arisen by selection. In the Shetland pony this type occurs with a largely white coat and coloured head, and with some other dark parts now and again. Such ponies are never described in the Shetland Pony Stud Book as pied, but as white with dark patches. Additionally one finds dominant piebald in the Shetland pony in the form of a dark coat with very little white, sometimes a single patch on the shoulder, back or ribs, or a particoloured mane and tail. These ponies too are not described in Britain as pied, even though the progeny of pied parents, but as dark with white patches.

Plate 15. Piebald. (*Photo:* Wiersma).

If the description is inaccurately given, this can lead to faulty conclusions, as is probably the case with Salisbury (1941) in his opinion that recessive piebald occurred in the American Shetland pony. In more that 7,000 matings of non-pied ponies, and ponies with small white markings, he found 2·4% of pied foals. White markings on head and legs, which are normally very rare among Shetlands, are chiefly seen in combination with piebald.

Walther (1913), assumed a factor E, while Wentworth assumed a factor P for piebald. Castle also acknowledges a factor P, Tuff and Berge a dominant allele of the S series, Odriozola a combination of genes from the S and W series. Comparison with a piebald in other species supports the hypothesis of the S gene. The gene for piebald operates on the cells of the neural crest, which expresses itself in sharply defined white areas.

Castle thinks that piebalds with very strong reduction of the dark parts, may be homozygote and that white-born-white in certain cases is to be thought of as a maximal form of piebaldness. The available data offer to date little support for this view though homozygote piebald horses do occur. The history of the Shetland Pony Stud Book shows only one single case of a white-born-white pony. That was in 1952 in the Isle of Unst, where a wholly white foal with dark eyes was born to pied parents. Whether in the Morocco Spotted Horse homozygote individuals occur, cannot be determined with certainty.

It is assumed provisionally, that piebald depends on a simple dominant gene that is epistatic to all other colour genes. There is insufficient foundation for the hypothesis that this gene is partially dominant in the sense that homozygotes give more white. Rather the impression is given that the extreme forms of piebald present the normal forms of variation that would be caused by a number of modifying genes. Hereby one could also regard the variation as the result of interaction with other genes, known as minor spotting genes (such as those which cause white markings on head and feet).

8:2 LEOPARD SPOTTED

Among coloured horses at the present day, spotted occupies an important position. According to Haines (1963) pictures of spotted

Plate 16. Leopard spotting. In the foal on the right, the spots can plainly be seen running in the direction of the hairs. (*Photo*: Wiersma).

horses dating from the 6th-century have been found in Persia and in Turkish miniatures and also in Chinese art. In the latter, from the 13th-century onwards, regular spotted horses are found depicted. The earliest European pictures date from the 12th-century. Flemish artists from the 15th-century onwards often painted spotted horses and these animals later became popular in France too (see the famous battle scene by A. van der Meulen *The French Army Under Louis XIV Crossing the Rhine*). J. Hamilton's painting (1727) of the stud at Lipizza is equally famous and shows spotted mares. It is presumed that spotted horses came from Asia via North Africa (Carthage) to Spain, and from there to other parts of Europe and to South America and Central America including Mexico from the early 16th-century. The diffusion in North American countries is historically well documented: at the beginning of the 18th-century the colour was known among the Nez Percé Indians, who later specialised in breeding spotted horses, now called Appaloosa in the United States, while

Pony of the Americas (POA) is a spotted pony breed of recent development.

Spotted individuals are still found today among some breeds of pony in Mongolia, Tibet, India and China, possibly also (they certainly were formerly) among the Akhal-Tekke breed of Turkestan. Up until 1930, spotted ponies were plentiful on the racecourse at Shanghai. In Europe, this colour still occurs in the Knabstrup horse of Denmark (Petersen, 1958), in the Pinzgau strain of Noriker in Austria and Bavaria, and sporadically in the latter day Andalusian. In America, Appaloosa breeding has taken a great upsurge.

Phenotypically, spotted presents a great range of variations, among which, however, four patterns can be discerned. (Hawkins, 1965).

Blanket pattern. Spotting confined to the croup, or to the entire hindquarter as far as the flanks. The pattern can consist of pale-grey, or white, with dark blotches and spots, which can sometimes be wanting. The rest of the coat is often ticked or roan, or can become so as the horse ages. Less frequent is the pattern of a normal whole coloured croup with white spots or a mixture of white and dark spots.

Leopard pattern. The classic form. The coat is wholly white, or very pale-roan, and covered with dark spots. The spots are round, or oval, often (and this goes for blanket-spotteds too) "dropping" in the direction of the hair, small and closely spaced on the neck and forehand, greater towards the rear. Apart from this, the spots may either be sharply outlined or fringed.

Snowflake pattern. The coat is sewn with little white, or roan, spots. Above all in this form, and notably in filly foals, it can happen that there are no spots at birth: they appear slowly, at first under the tail and on the head (nose and mouth).

Mottled pattern. The coat is most often irregularly ticked with white, having also large or small roan spots, their outlines rather blurred. Sometimes also a coat looking like ordinary roan, but in which dark blots appear.

Other patterns and shades are chiefly mixed forms of the above, such as a coat with dark and light spots, or a fluid transition between blanket and leopard pattern. In the Appaloosa, striped hoofs are often seen with a spotted skin, especially round the eyes, mouth, nose and genitalia. Ring eyes, in which the pigment in the conjunctiva round the cornea is deficient, and the white colour of the sclera extends to the edge of the cornea, is a further characteristic to which great value is attached.

Little is, as yet, known genetically about leopard spotting. Odriozola postulates an allele of the W series, in combination, or not, with an S allele. Llewellyn (1949) also assumes two factors: one (compare with the R gene) influencing pigment formation in individual hairs; the other operating on the distribution of pigmented and achromatic hairs (the Appaloosa factor). The effect may be unilaterally complementary (at least in leopard spotting all over the coat) in the sense that the roaning factor can come to expression without the

Plate 17. Blanket spotted foal. The dam is pronounced roan with some spots on the hindquarters. (*Photo:* Wiersma).

84

Plate 18. Combination of piebald and blanket spotting in a foal of a piebald dam. (*Photo*: Wiersma).

Appaloosa factor, but not *vice versa*. The Appaloosa factor, which gathers the coloured hairs together in small centres (or lets them remain in such) may thus be carried invisibly. The roan factor in question is not identical with the ordinary R factor.

The stud book does not recommend the mating roan to Appaloosa, because it is apparent that the R factor also attacks the spots of pigmented hairs. Thereby much of the contrast in the coat is lost. Sometimes the appearance of spots is completely suppressed (Hatley, 1962). The same is true of the G factor: leopard spotted horses carrying the factor will turn white all over.

The more recent view of Jones (1971) is equipped with more arguments, depending on at least three dominant, and, preferably, two recessive factors, which may all be homologous with piebald factors known in mice. Jones establishes that pigment is influenced in two ways: in the first place by a loss in confined areas of small specks, or even in larger areas of white without sharply defined borders; and in the second place by an increase in other, almost always, sharply defined spots. On these grounds, he assumes an allele of the W series, W^{ap} which is strongly expressive and gives a white coat with coloured spots. The occurrence of these spots takes place through distribution of locally surviving melanocytes, which do not migrate further into their surroundings. The occasional occurrence of scanty mane and tail (rat's tail) may be a pleiotropic effect of the W^{ap} allele.

An allele of the Sl (for steel) series may also be present, which in mice has an effect near enough identical with that of the W gene. The Sl^{ap} gene, which actually produces little white spots, can also cause a white coat all over with dark spots. For the occurrence of whole, or partly roan coats, Jones assumes the R^{ap} gene, which is not supposed to give any spots at all, unless in combination with W^{ap} or Sl^{ap}.

The expression of these three principal genes is strongly influenced by a number of modifiers that cannot be closely identified, which normally can be invisibly carried, so that the diffusion of the Appaloosa pattern acquires a quantative character. Its isolation identifies the very strongly modifying gene M, which may give the typical characteristics of white sclera, spotted skin and striped hoofs. (Spotted skin on the mouth, eyes, ears and genitalia is also seen in other breeds, including the Arab and Lipizzan.)

The two recessive genes are the f (flexed tail) and the blo (blotch) genes.

The f gene in mice gives in homozygote form, white spots and aberrations of the caudal vertebrae (fusions and kinks between vertebrae). A kink in the tail is sometimes also found in the Appaloosa. Besides, the f gene in the presence of a sufficient number of modifying genes may give a slight blanket spotted effect.

The blo gene would lead to an aberrant form of spots. In mice it causes a certain dilution of pigment, similar to chinchilla, but in irregular patches. In essence, this factor attacks the development of the hair in certain places. The aberrant hair seems to form an aberrant environment for the melanocyte in the hair bulbs, which results in changes of colour. It is possible that the blo gene in combination with other Appaloosa factors acts as a modifier.

Granted the above concept, one can set up, schematically, the accompanying conspectus of Appaloosa genotypes and phenotypes. In it, the degree of effectiveness of the whole complex of modifiers is indicated throughout by + (plus) signs (*see Table 3*).

From this summary, it appears that almost equal phenotypes can result from different genes and combinations of genes. From which it follows that it is hard in practice to prognosticate the result of a given mating, or even to produce a pattern that will breed true, if indeed this is possible, in view of the strongly quantitative character of the Appaloosa pattern. This means that the result of most matings will be a surprise, although leopard spotted × leopard spotted offers the highest chances of leopard spotted and/or blanket spotted off-spring.

This exposition must, above all, be seen as an example of a train of thought from comparative genetics. One arrives at such a concept by proceeding by analogy with genes in other species: genes which in dogs give forms of leopard spots, as for instance the combination of the T (ticking) gene, and alleles from the S series (Dalmation dogs, genotype TTs^ws^w) or of the M (Merle or dapple) factor and alleles of the S series (Harlequin Great Dane).

Finally, let it be remarked that in the Appaloosa, sometimes a displacement, magnification or diminuition of spots occur, which, according to Jones, is an indication that even in the adult lifetime of the animal, migration of melanoblasts is possible. This is connected with the remarkable fact that about 20% of Appaloosa foals are born without the typical coat markings, while the white sclera is present at birth and in almost a third of the foals the spotted skin also. In the remainder, this characteristic develops between the first and third years of life. During this period, the marks on the coat can also appear. This mostly begins with little tufts of white hair which grow into grey or white patches, or to larger areas, in which darker spots then form. It can also happen that in a light-roan coat, or one that is all but white, coloured patches can appear later. Besides this, leopard spotting seems to be influenced by sex, probably by hormones, since most stallions colour up faster and with more contrast than mares.

As regards the connection with other forms of spotting, it should be noted that leopard pattern can be seen on the same coat as pie-bald, and even together with the intermediary known as sabino

87

TABLE 3

Conspectus of genotypes and phenotypes in the Spotted Horse

Genotype	Modifiers	Phenotype
W^{ap} __	+	Blanket pattern with clear-cut coloured spots.
W^{ap} __	+ +	Extension of the blanket forwards; intermediary form between blanket and leopard, in which the head, neck and forehand are still whole-coloured.
W^{ap} __	+ + +	Leopard pattern; all white coat with dark spots.
$W^{ap}W^{ap}$	+	Blanket pattern with spots.
$W^{ap}W^{ap}$	+ +	Leopard pattern.
$W^{ap}W^{ap}$	+ + +	Leopard pattern.
Sl^{ap} __	+ + +	Irregular unevenly roaned coat, mainly on the hindquarters and back, without plain spots; coat gives varnished effect, hence American term "varnished roan".
Sl^{ap} __	+ + +	Light roan to white blanket with indistinct roan edges, shading-off. Hoar-frost effect.
$Sl^{ap}Sl^{ap}$	+	Irregular roan on forehand, shading off behind into indistinctly bordered, very light roan coat.
$Sl^{ap}Sl^{ap}$	+ +	Almost entirely light roan, but not quite white, with a few dark spots.
$Sl^{ap}Sl^{ap}$	+ + +	Leopard pattern.
Rn^{ap}-	+	Some roan to white spots about the hindquarters.
Rn^{ap}-	+ +	Ditto; the white spots can run together slightly.
Rn^{ap}-	+ + +	White, very sharply defined blanket.
$Rn^{ap}Rn^{ap}$	+	Light roan coat with strongly roaned to white patches.
$Rn^{ap}Rn^{ap}$	+ +	Roan coat with extension of the white in which dark spots can also appear.
$Rn^{ap}Rn^{ap}$	+ + +	All white coat over hindquarters and thigh; may extend forward as far as the shoulder but no dark spots.

W^{ap}-Sl^{ap} __

W^{ap}-Rn^{ap}— + to + + +Leopard pattern

Sl^{ap}-Rn^{ap} __

which will be dealt with later. According to von Lehmann (1951), what is known as Argentine Pied, or Chubari, is a form of leopard pattern, or in any case nearly related to it. Chubari consists of a very pronounced roan, or grey, coat with a freakish pattern of ill defined white spots all over the coat. Odriozola places leopard spotting and Chubari in one group to which piebald would also belong. He represents the respective genotypes as W'S, WS, and W"S, meaning thereby to imply by the W symbols not a rationing of alleles, but simply other positions of the W gene in the chromosome. The different phenotypes should thus be thought of as effects of position by displacement of the W locus (after an inversion within the chromosome).

8:3 SPLASHED-WHITE

This form of recessive spotting, which occurs in the Finnish horse among other breeds, has been investigated by Klemola (1930, 1933), and the designation "splashed-white" is his coining. The phenotype differs from piebald and skewbald mainly by a different distribution of the white. This spreads itself out in patches, or areas from the ventral region of the body upwards, and out over the back, ribs, neck and head. The patches are mostly large and the head is often white all over. Klemola points out that in a comparison he made of some ten different patterns of piebald and splashed-white with increasing expansion of the white parts, especially in the more extreme forms, it appeared strongly that parts which in dominant pied are white, in recessive pied are coloured, and vice versa. While it does appear that splashed-white horses always have glass eyes (with light grey, or nacreous iris) it is not known whether, in splashed-white, a phenotype can be thrown up, in which the coat is white all over, nor do we know what the relationship is between this and other kinds of white spotting.

But glass eyes do also occur separately, in the proportion "splashed is to glass eyes, as three is to one". But if one takes into account the progeny of animals that are heterozygote for this pied factor, then the proportion would be one to one.

It is on this that Klemola bases his theory that both splashed white and glass eyes are caused by two pairs of recessive genes in the S series, which possibly have such a dominance relationship that the factor for splashed-white (s^2) is hypostatic *vis-a-vis* the factor for glass eyes (s^1). Heterozygotes (s^1s^2) would have exclusively glass eyes. But it is also possible that both characteristics proceed from one and the same genotype, based on only one pair of genes. As against this, Klemola adduces that glass eyes are also found in other breeds, independent of white spotting. A well known example of splashed-white was the Finnish stallion Eversti, who had glass eyes and big, but ordinary looking, white marks on his head and legs; he got 62 progeny with glass eyes, of which 16 were also pied; and a further 11 progeny with normal eyes whose foals, however, had glass eyes; and 5 of them had splashed-white foals. Of these last, 19 progeny are known to have had glass eyes, and 10 of them were pied.

According to von Lehmann, splashed-white occurs sporadically in other North European heavy breeds. The occasional appearance

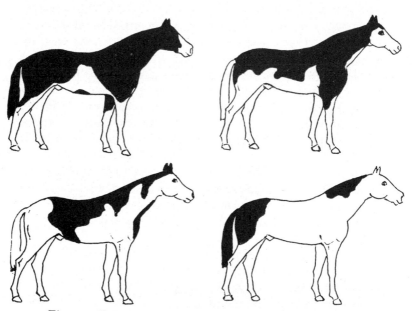

Figure 5. Expansion of the white areas in some phenotypes of splashed white.

of pied foals in the Welsh pony could also be recessive spotting. A recent case is of a foal born in Holland in 1972: it was a colt, and had very large white patches. From its pedigree it appears that the dam of his granddam once had a pied foal too.

8:4 OVERO

It is assumed that among American pied horses (generally called pintos) recessive white spotting also occurs, which are known as Overo variety. This is something different again from splashed-white, and the pattern is generally less regular than in piebald (*tobiano*). The white areas and patches are mostly very capriciously shaped with ramifications and indented edges, coming up from under the belly, and spreading all over the coat, also on the head and neck. In these horses, the back is usually dark coloured. There is great variation in the phenotype even among overos. Still, the general impression is clearly different from piebald. On these grounds, overo is regarded as a separate, recessive form of white spotting also found among horses in Latin America where it is known as pampo baixo.

Odriozola explains this by recessive alleles of the S series. A similar, perhaps even identical, form of spotting occurs in various North African breeds, including the "Dongola Barb" of the Sudan and Ethiopia, and the ordinary country bred horse of Nigeria.

The factors for overo and piebald show possible interaction. Horses carrying both factors have a predominantly white coat, with only here and there a dark patch.

Jones counts the white spots that are seen on the belly of Hackneys and the larger white marks on the legs and belly of Clydesdales as overo. But, there are phenotypical differences in the last named breed. There has, as yet, been no detailed enquiry into the recessive nature of overo. Therefore we should provisionally assign the Clydes-dale markings to a separate form and deal with it in the next section, under Sabino. A very constant characteristic in the Clydesdale is white marks high up the leg and much white about the head. From the fact that this breed forms a small, close knit population in the U.S.A. (where pied coats are very common) and that some imported sires from whom there has been much inbreeding had white under

Figure 6. Expansion of the white areas in some overo phenotypes.

the belly, we are not justified in the assumption that we have here a recessive factor, for lack of more exact data. The impression is rather that there is a dominant principal gene, and that the expansion of white is dependent on a number of modifiers.

All white foals can be born of parents who are overo with much white. In that case there are a great number of modifiers which, as pleiotropic (side) effects, produce certain aberrations, such as atresia coli (congenital occlusions, or serious narrowing of the large intestine) and haemolytic anaemia (breakdown of red corpuscles). These foals die soon after birth. This condition is known as "white colt syndrome". On the grounds of these side effects, Jones thinks that the overo factor may be a W allele. It might be desirable to investigate a possible allelism with the splashed-white factor.

8:5 SABINO

This is an American expression, meaning a kind of piebald with often indistinct and irregularly bordered white radiating from under the breast, the belly and the extremities, and thence spreading laterally up the ribs and sometimes to other parts of the body. The rest of the coat is often ticked with white, or roan.

On closer examination this form of white spotting seems not uncommon and to be present in several breeds, even in Europe. American light horse breeds include the Tennessee Walking Horse, and the Missouri Foxtrotting Horse. It is found in Europe in the pre-war studs of East and West Prussia, the Hanoverian, the Holsteiner, the Westphalian Light Horse, the Dutch Light Horse and even in heavy breeds like the Clydesdale and, in a lesser degree, the Shire.

The Sabino pattern can be conspicuously studied in the Dutch Light Horse, both in the Groningen and the Gelderland breeds, in which it has occurred from of old, especially in the horse breeding district of Drenthe. The phenotype exhibits a similar variation to that of overo, but in not nearly such a spectacular form. One finds horses with not very conspicuous markings, such as a patch on the belly, a spot on the knee, or on the foreside of the hock, and more diffuse white on the legs such as a white stocking or boot, often running up in front. This is, above all, typical on the forelegs, where

Plate 19. Sabino, or O, factor piebald; a frequently occuring phenotype.

93

normally white high up is not so common. Concurrently one finds horses with diffuse irregular patches under the belly and breast, sometimes also all over the coat, so that the appearance is virtually that of piebald.

Most frequently, but not in all cases, the coat is roan or ticked (hence the popular name Drenthe Blue). It may even be the sole indication of the presence of the Sabino factor. The impression persists that the markings on the head are, on the whole, larger than usual, and often extend down to the underlip and throat. All in all, these horses, in populations where marks are small and sparse, are conspicuous by their markings of the kind associated with piebald.

In Holland, the number of these horses has somewhat increased in the last few decades, due to the fact that five stallions with the sabino factor have been standing at stud, mostly in the V.L.N. district. Among mares entered in the V.L.N. Stud Book between 1953 and 1958, Sabino seemed to occur in 0·6% of the Groningen type and in 1·8% of the Gelderland type. As to their pedigree, they were daughters of the stallion Noorderlicht 1318 NWP, and of the spotted stallion Jotham 1054 Sgldt and Oleander 1091 Sgldt.

They belonged to families that all traced back to a daughter of the stallion Primo 303 Nstg, and Jaffino 523 Sgrt. Primo is registered as roan, Jaffino and Nooderlicht were ticked with markings high up the leg. Jotham was chestnut, ticked white, with a big white patch under the belly and a patch on the croup. The official description of his son Oleander runs: Golden-chestnut, very wide blaze running right down into both nostrils, white underlip and under jaw; both forelegs booted; stocking left hind very high in front, irregular; sock right hind running up very irregularly in front to the knee; white belly with chestnut patches, white patch on ribs near side.

Distinctly pied foals by all these stallions are known, but they were only registered as such when it was a question of large white patches all over the body. This phenotype occurred in 18·2% of Sabino coloured mares, while 59·4% had patches only under the belly and 34% had one, or more, patches somewhere else on the coat. Sixty-six per cent of them were registered as ticked, or roan, but of the mares that were registered as pied, 90% had this characteristic.

There has been no penetrating research on Sabino yet. As against

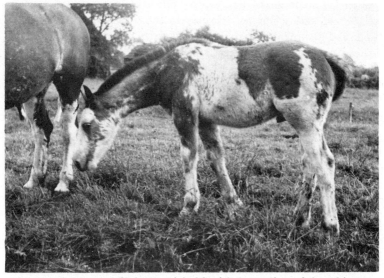

Plate 20. Sabino, or O, factor piebald with expansion of the white areas in a foal out of a sabino mare. (*Photo*: Wiersma).

Klemola who calls it a recessivé form of white spotting (1933), Wiersma (1961) thinks it is a question of a dominant gene, which he associates with an O (depigmentation) factor, which in the homozygote condition can cause a wholly, or almost wholly, white coat. Even before the foundation of the Dutch stud books it was known that white foals could be born to (both) sabino parents. Some breeders deliberately bred to this end. These white-born foals have dark, but also some have blue, eyes and sometimes some dim blue spots, or some pigmented hairs in the head or in the ears. The above named stallions have also got white born foals. Wiersma's submission that the sabino factor is simply dominant (forming intermediary characteristics) seems to be supported by the observation that in families tracing back in tail female several generations in which this factor runs, not a single generation is passed over, and that approximately equal numbers of sabino, and non-sabino foals are born. The one-to-one ratio is however hard to test, due to the great variability of phenotype and the recognition of the sabino factor in doubtful cases, when progeny are lacking.

Von Lehmann also (1941, 1951) who made comparative studies of piebald and white born horses in some West Prussian studs, assumes a dominant factor from the W series that can result as easily in roan as in piebald when it is heterozygote; what is called intermediary piebald. Moreover he points to a possible connection with the white-born horses formerly bred at the studs of Herrenhausen in Saxony, and Frederiksborg in Denmark (Wriedt, 1918, 1924). On the basis of the phenotype, one could indeed think of a W or S allele occurring as a principal gene, or a combination of both, strongly influenced in expression by modifying genes. One is also put in mind of the homology with other genes, *e.g.* the Sp (splotch) gene in mice.

Plate 21. An extensively pied sabino mare, with her sabino foal (by a whole-coloured sire). The darker patches on the mare are roan.

(*Photo:* Wiersma)

96

These hypotheses do not serve directly to explain why a phenotype like sabino can suddenly arise from the mating of self coloured parents and then be dominantly inherited. Such, for instance, was the case in 1946 with the Standard Bred Trotter, King Majesty, whose sire was black, and his dam bay; he was registered as roan, with a wide blaze right down, but in fact he was sabino, for he sired several pied foals. Von Lehmann explains this by crossing over, in his observations on like cases, of certain factors. Cases confirmed among Dutch Light Horses, however, are rather too numerous to deduce their cause from mutative alterations, however bizarre, unless a certain locus (W?) is very sensitive to this. Rather, one is led to think of an additive effect of what are called, minor spotting genes. As these occur singly, or in small numbers, in the genotype, they have a low degree of penetration and do not result in very striking markings. It is also possible that in a given genotype, the interaction of genes is such that the presence of certain spotting genes makes the expression of other spotting genes stronger.

Be that as it may, it is a fact that in certain gene combinations, what are called minor spotting genes, against which in Holland there has never been any selective breeding anyway, can produce an extensively piebald phenotype. But mostly, their expression has been confined to one, or more, spots on the coat. These spots are often found ventrally, around the navel, but also between the legs, on the ribs, neck, and elsewhere on the coat. Sometimes they are more widespread, so that the registration certificate reads "tiger marks between thighs". Such markings are encountered regularly in increasing measure over the years among horses of the Gelderland type (in a good 5% of mares registered in the V.L.N. Stud Book). These horses did not belong to the typical sabino families mentioned above, and in more than 90% of cases, the parents had no such markings. The various stallions also, who had spots on the belly and have stood at stud over the years, seem only to have passed on the characteristic to one single foal. So the inheritance may be recessive, but just as well dominant with a low and variable degree of penetration.

The relationship, too, with the extensive sabino phenotype is unclear. Possibly, we have here a complex of modifiers, making up part of the sabino genotype. In either case, the impression persists

Plate 22. Heavily ticked white or roan under the belly, and in the stifle; this is the picture associated with the O factor. (*Photo*: Wiersma)

that spots on the belly can arise, quite apart from the identical phenotype within the sabino group of pied horses.

In Hackneys equally, the above named small spots have always been present. The famous stallion Black Magic of Nork 15087 HSB, himself spotted in the stifle, and above the right knee, got several foals with a spot on the belly, sometimes linked with slight ticking in the stifle. In Dutch breeding, it was the stallions Alethorpe Admiral 127 Nstg, and his son, Emigrant 102 Nstg (who had no conspicuous marks himself) that more than once sired these markings, and, in some cases, even a sabino type phenotype. One may guess that even the Hackney Hockwold Cadet I GPS registered as strawberry roan belonged to the sabino group. Many of his roan progeny (*e.g.* his son Feu Sacré 40 GPS), had very strange and capricious markings.

Further, as to white born out of sabino parents; very few data are available about the results of mating white-born to white-born or white-born to whole colour. So far as is known, no white-born stallion has ever stood at stud officially in Holland. The number of registered white-born foals is moreover, too small for reliable research. Maybe white-born arises from a combination of homozygosis of a principal gene, and a maximum of modifiers (that is, if one subscribes to the hypotheses of dominance).

A recent case (Wiersma, 1961) is the white-born mare Sneeuwwitje 28362 NWP, who mated to whole coloured horses, threw three white born, one intermediary (roan) and two whole coloured foals, whereas what was expected was six sabinos. Thus, heterozygotes can be white too, assuming that Sneeuwwitje is really sabino pied. Actually her sire was bay, and her dam grey (G), and the latter, both phenotypically and in the light of the colour of her others foals, gave not a single indication that she possessed the sabino factor. We have also heard of a foal, born white in the 1920s, by the well known Colonel NSTg.31 H (ticked chestnut with four white socks) out of a sabino dam Dartha 2150 NsTg.

Documentary sources do not record whether white-born foals have been thrown up in Clydesdale breeding. In this breed, one finds besides roan pronounced spotted coats, with capriciously shaped white areas, coming up between the forelegs and up the neck. This is true also of Westphalian breeding, in which at least two sabino pied horses have stood at stud. These were Sonnenschein 846, tracing back to Schlütter, foaled in 1928: he got very many pied foals; and Morheus 836, of the Prussian Morgenstern line, foaled in 1927, whose sire and grandsire were sabino (Haselon 1941).

Cases like Sneeuwwitje, born white of whole coloured parents, in which most people assume a relationship with intermediary piebald, are often documented. Thus, in 1943, a chestnut sire and a bay dam of the Belgian Draught breed, threw a white foal with blue eyes; and in 1950, a roan sire and a dark-bay dam, of the same breed, threw a white foal with dark eyes, white hoofs and some ruddy hairs on the dock, in the forelock, on the ears and on the croup. The most recent case is of the bay parents Murghab and Tharsine in France in 1963, whose foal Mont Blanc II was born white. This Thoroughbred colt has been kept entire and in the foaling season of 1970 one of his foals was born white. Although these isolated cases may arise from muta-

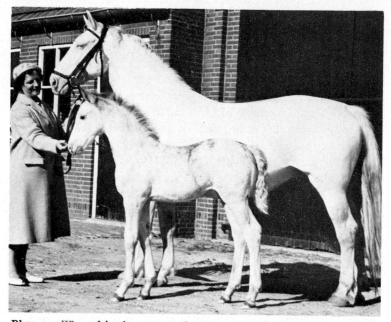

Plate 23. The white-born mare Sneeuwwitje, with blue eyes and pink skin and her blue-roan foal, sabino (with dark skin and dark eyes) by a black sire. (*Photo:* Wiersma).

tion, it is still possible that non-genétic causes may have led to the failure of migration, or proliferation, of the melanoblasts.

8:6 DOMINANT WHITE

Among white-born horses are reckoned the so called albino horses, which are deliberately bred in some parts, including Nebraska in America. Since 1937, there has been an American Albino Horse Club, with a stud book. These horses are white all over: very rarely there is a dark spot. So the skin is pink, and without pigmentation, as are the hoofs. The eyes are blue, or hazel.

Salisbury and Castle call these horses dominant white, the factor for it being a W allele. From the researches of Pulos and Hutt (1969), it appears that dominant white never breeds true, and thus can only occur in heterozygote form (Ww). Two dominant white parents can throw whole coloured foals, or white foals, in the proportion of two white to one of another colour. This proportion proves that there are no homozygotes. In homozygote form, the factor for dominant white is crypto-lethal, meaning that the homozygote embryos die at such an early stage of pregnancy that their presence is not suspected. In this connection, Jones preferred to use the symbol L^w, in accordance with the modern convention for lethal factors, since no homology with delayed lethal, or semi-lethal, W alleles in mice can be established. Comparison with the white born horses of the erstwhile Frederiksborg Stud suggests itself. But, according to Wriedt, the factor for white was there linked with a lethal gene.

Plate 24. Skjevet; a form of piebald peculiar to the Fjord horse.

8:7 SKJEVET ("Skew")

A unique form of spotting with large white marks is found in Norway, among certain strains of Fjord horses. It is known as skjevet (= oblique stripe). It always consists of an irregularly bordered oblong white patch, running diagonally from the neck over the wither and the shoulder downwards, sometimes being linked with some isolated spots on the back and ribs.

In coats so marked, one not infrequently finds white ticking and white on the legs. In these strains, there are also cases of ticked, or roan, coats without white marks. Sometimes, the marks are said to grow larger during life. Berge (1963) assumes for this form of white spotting, a dominant allele of the S series, namely S^g.

8:8 WHITE MARKS

Marks on the head and legs are very common, and show, with more or less unvarying location, a varying extent (*see Chapter 1:8*). They are caused through minor spotting genes.

Numerous studies have already been made of heritability and inheritance of such marks. Walther (1913) pointed out that they happened oftener with chestnut ground colour than with bay or black, and further, that there was an obvious correlation between markings on the head and those on the legs, which Briquet (1957) confirmed. Markings are more frequent on the hind, than on the forelegs, besides which there is a decided tendency to the left side (Dreux 1968). Ermine marks (widespread among light horse breeds, even in Holland) found mostly about the coronet and pastern, would be caused according to Jones, by a dominant factor known as D^1 (distal leg spot).

All researchers came to different conclusions about heritability. This is probably connected with differences in gene frequency, and in modifiers in different breeds.

Salisbury postulates not only dominant, but also recessive forms of white markings. Blunn and Howell (1936) discovered among a small population of Arabs, that stars, narrow races and snips were dominantly inherited, and that marks on the lips and chin were, on the contrary, part of a recessive inheritance pattern. Dreux deduced from an extensive phenotypical research programme on French trotters, that markings on the head can issue from two centres, one in the forehead and another round the nose and upper lip. A series of markings is developed from each of these centres and when they occur simultaneously and extend towards each other so as to grow together, the result is a blaze running right down. Furthermore, Dreux points to a possible additive effect in the factors for markings on the face, when he notes that mating of star to star often gives rise to larger markings (blazes).

TABLE 4
Conspectus of Piebald factors

Pattern, etc.	Castle	Odrio-zola	Kle-mola	Berge	Jones
Pied (tobiano)	P	W"S		S	T
Spotted		W'S			W^{ap}, Sl^{ap},
Chubari		WS			Rn^{ap}
Splashed-white			s^1, s^2		
Overo					W
Recessive Pied (pampo baixo)		ss			
White Markings				S & s	
Skjevet				S^g	
Dominant White	W	W			L^w

From experiments by Geurts (1969) on the Friesian horse, a breed in which for many years past there has been a selection against large white marks on the head, these would appear still to occur in only 13% of individuals and to be, for the most part, small or very small. Although the impression remains that such marks are recessive, this cannot be proved, and a dominant inheritance with incomplete penetration seems more likely.

It is generally assumed that white markings are caused by alleles of the S series, which are influenced in their expression by a number of modifying genes, so that the inheritance acquires more of a multi-factorial character. A conspectus of the factor symbols used by different students of this phenomenon is given in Table 4.

BIBLIOGRAPHY

Arabian Horse Registry of America (A.H.R.), 1970. Identifying the arabian. Englewood, Colorado.

Barkema, R., 1970. De valen van Eendenoord. Tijdschr. Diergeneesk. 95: 753.

Berge, S., 1963. Heste fargenes Genetikk. Tidsskr. Norske Landbr. 70: 359–410.

Blunn, C. & C. Howell, 1936. The inheritance of white facial markings in Arab horses. J. Hered. 27: 293–299.

Briquet, R., 1952. Os chamados cavalos albinos. Bolm ind. anim. 1.

Briquet, R., 1957. Genetica da pelagem do cavalo. Monogr. Inst. Zootecn. Rio de J. I.

Castle, W., 1940a. Mammalian genetics. Cambridge.

Castle, W., 1940b. The genetics of coat color in horses. J. Hered. 31: 127–128.

Castle, W., 1942. The ABC of color inheritance in horses. J. Hered. 33: 23–25.

Castle, W., 1946. Genetics of the Palomino horse. J. Hered. 37: 35–38.

Castle, W., 1951. Dominant and recessive black in mammals. J. Hered. 42: 48–50.

Castle, W., 1952. The eumelanine horse: black or brown. J. Hered. 43: 68.

Castle, W., 1954. Coat colour inheritance in horses and in other animals. Genetics 39: 35–44.

Castle, W., 1961. The genetics of the claybank-dun horse. J. Hered. 52: 121–122.

Castle, W. & F. King, 1951. New evidence of the genetics of the Palomino horse. J. Hered. 42: 61–64.

Castle, W. & W. Singleton, 1960. Genetics of the brown horse. J. Hered. 51: 127–131.

Castle, W. & W. Singleton, 1961. The Palomino horse. Genetics 46: 1143–1150.

Castle, W. & F. Smith, 1953. Silver dapple, a unique color variety among Shetland ponies. J. Hered. 44: 139–146.

Crew, F. & B. A. Smith, 1930. The genetics of the horse. Biblthca genet. 6: 123–170.

Domanski, A. & R. Prawochenski, 1948. Dun coat colours in horses. J. Hered. 39: 367–371.

Domingues, O., 1941. A pelagem tobiana ou pampa no Brasil. Bolm Soc. bras. Agron. 4: 409–414.

Dreux, Ph., 1966. Introduction statistique à la génétique des marques blanches limitées chez le cheval. Annls Génét. 9: 66–72.

Geurts, R. 1969. Genetische analyse en structuur van de fokkerij van het Friese paard. Thesis Maastricht.

Gremmel, Fr., 1939. Coat colors in horses, J. Hered. 30: 437–445.

Hagedoorn, A. & F. van der Molen, 1934. Rode en vale kleur bij onze Nederlandse runderen. De nieuwe Veldbode 1: 787.

Haines, Fr., 1963. Appaloosa, the spotted horse in art and history. University Texas, Austin.

Haselon, B., 1941. Die wichtigsten Hengstlinien der Westfälischen Warmblutzucht. Thesis. Bonn.

Hatley, G., 1962. Crosses that will kill your color. Appaloosa News 19, nr.2.

Hawkins, R., 1965. The Appaloosa, breed characteristics. Hawkins & Hubbell, Riverside, California.

Homan, H., 1952. De vererving van de isabelkleur bij paarden. Landbouwk. Tijdschr. 64: 770–778.

Ibsen, H., 1933. Cattle inheritance. I: Color. Genetics 18: 441–480.

Isenbart, H., 1969. Das Königreich des Pferdes., Bucher, Luzern.

Jones, W., 1971. Appaloosa color inheritance. Appaloosa News 28, nr. 1: 26–30.

Jones, W. & R. Bogart, 1971. Genetics of the horse. Caballus publ., East Lansing, Michigan.

Klemola, V., 1930. Uber die Morphologie und Vererbung der dominanten und recessieven Scheckung sowie der Glasaugigkeit beim Pferde. Z. Zücht. 20: 24–78.

Klemola, V., 1933. The pied and splashed white patterns in horses and ponies. J. Hered. 24: 65–69.

Krumbiegel, I., 1958. Einhufer. Ziemsen, Wittenberg.

Lauvergne, J., 1966. Génétique de la couleur du pelage des boivins domestiques. Biblthca Genet. 20: 1–68.

Lehmann, E. von, 1941. Beiträge zur Vererbung weiszgeborener Pferde. Z. Zücht. 49: 191–195.

Lehmann, E. von, 1951. Die Iris und die Rumpfscheckung beim Pferd. Z. Zücht, 59.

Lexique International, 1972. uitg. v. la Société d'encouragement pour l'amélioration des races de chevaux en France. Pailhé, Paris.

Llewellyn, Ph., 1949. The British spotted horse. Riding 8, nr. 11.

Loen, J., 1939. Farge-Nedarvinga hos Vestlandhesten. Stamb. Vestl. Hest. 11: 1–52.

Marrero y Galindez, A., 1945. Cromohipologia. Edition del autor, Buenos Aires.

McCann, L., 1916. Sorrel colour in horses. J. Hered. 7: 370–372.

Merkens, J., 1953. De vererving van de haarkleur bij paarden. Tijdschr. Diergeneesk. 78: 189–215.

Meyer, E., 1949. Farbe und Abzeichen bei Pferden. Schaper, Hannover.

Mohr, E., 1959. Das Urwildpferd. Ziemsen, Wittenberg.

Munckel, H., 1929. Untersuchungen über Farben und Abzeichen der Pferde und ihre Vererbung. Z. Zücht. 16: 1–200.

Munckel, H., 1934. Ergänzende Untersuchungen über die Abzeichen der Pferde und ihre Vererbung. Z. Zücht. 30: 65–114.

Nordang, J., 1955. Hestealet på Vestlandet i nyare tid. J. N. Minnefond, Bergen.

Norton, D., 1949. The Palomino horse, Bordon, Los Angeles.

Odriozola, M., 1951. A los colores del caballo. Publnes Sind. nac. Ganaderia, Madrid.

Papendieck, L., 1957. Das Kleinpferd. Pary, Hamburg.

Pedersen, A., 1954. Lidt om knapstrupperne. Arsskr. K. Landbr. Hojsk. For. Odense.

Pulos, W. & F. Hutt, 1969. Lethal dominant white in horses. J. Hered. 60: 59–64.

Punnett, R., 1930. On the series of allelomorphs connected with the production of black pigment in rabbits. J. Genet. 23: 265–274.

Salisbury, G. & J. Britton, 1941a. The inheritance of equine coat color. I: The basic colors and patterns. J. Hered. 32: 235–240.

Salisbury, G. & J. Britton, 1941b. The inheritance of equine coat color. II: The dilutes. J. Hered. 32: 255–260.

Sänger, O., 1962. Farbabweichungen bei Fohlengeburten. Kleinpferdezucht. 10. nr. 34.

Searle, A., 1968. Comparative genetics of coat colour in mammals. Logos, London.

Singleton, R., 1969. The genetics of mammalian coat color. J. Hered. 60: 25–26.

Singleton, R. & Q. Bond, 1966. A allele necessary for dilute coat color in horses. J. Hered. 57: 75–77.

Smith, A., 1925. A study of the inheritance of certain color characters in the Shorthorn breed. J. Hered. 16: 73–84.

Spoelstra, W., 1946. Kleur en kenbare tekens van paarden. N.W.P. publication, Leeuwarden.

Ströver, A., 1917. Die Vererbung der Haarfarben beim Vollblutpferde. Schaper, Hannover.

Sturtevant, A., 1912. A critical examination of recent studies in color inheritance in horses. J. Hered. 2: 41–52.

Tuff, P., 1933. Genetiske undersøkelser over hestefarver. Proc. 4 th Nord. Vet. Kongr. 689–716.

Walther, A., 1912a. Beiträge zur Kenntnis der Vererbung der Pferdefarben. Schaper, Hannover.

Walther, A., 1912b. Studien uber Vererbung bei Pferden. I: Die Vererbung des schwarzen Pigments. Z. indukt. Abstamm. VererbLehre 6: 238–244.

Walther, A., 1913. Die Vererbung unpigmentierter Haare und Hautstellen bei Rind und Pferd. Z. indukt. Abstamm. VererbLehre 10: 1–48.

Wentworth, E., 1914. Color inheritance in the horse. Z. indukt. Abstamm. VererbLehre 11: 10–17.

Wiersema, J., 1955. Het verschijnen van de isabelkleur bij warmbloedpaarden in Nederland. Paard 23: nr. 1: 1–4.

Wiersema, J., 1961a. De haarkleur der paarden I. Paard 28: nr. 17: 1–6.

Wiersema, J., 1961b. De haarkleur der paarden III. Paard 29: nr. 6: 2–4.

Wiersema, J., 1961c. De haarkleur der paarden IV. Paard 29: nr. 10: 5–6.

Wilson, J., 1912. The inheritance of the dun coat colour in horses. Proc. R. Ir. Acad. 13: 184–201.

Wolning, W. & Th. de Groot, 1935. De haarkleur bij paarden. Nieuwe Veldbode 2, nr. 42: 13–15.

Wriedt, Chr., 1924. Vererbungsfaktoren bei weiszen Pferden im Gestüt Frederiksborg. Z. Zücht. 1: 231–242.

Wriedt, Chr., 1925. Vererbungsuntersuchungen beim Pferd. Z. indukt. Abstamm. VererbLehre 37: 88–101.

Wriedt, Chr., 1928. Arv af farve hos hest. Tidsskr. Norske Landbr. 35: 297–329.

Wriedt, Chr. & E. Mohr., 1918. Albinisme in hester. Tidsskr. Norske Landbr. 25: 396–404.

Wright, S., 1917. Color inheritance in mammals. J. Hered. 8: 560–564.

Züblin, H., 1947. Wesen und Uraschen der Schimmelbildung beim Pferd. Thesis, Bern.